John Stevens Cabot Abbott, James Fowler Simmons

South and North

Or, impressions received during a trip to Cuba and the South

John Stevens Cabot Abbott, James Fowler Simmons

South and North

Or, impressions received during a trip to Cuba and the South

ISBN/EAN: 9783337149406

Printed in Europe, USA, Canada, Australia, Japan

Cover: Foto ©Andreas Hilbeck / pixelio.de

More available books at **www.hansebooks.com**

SOUTH AND NORTH;

OR,

IMPRESSIONS RECEIVED DURING A TRIP TO CUBA AND THE SOUTH.

BY JOHN S. C. ABBOTT.

"For freedom's battle, once begun,
Bequeathed from bleeding sire to son,
Though baffled oft, is ever won."

New-York:
ABBEY & ABBOT,
119 NASSAU STREET.
1860.

ENTERED, according to Act of Congress, in the year 1860, by
ABBEY & ABBOT,
in the Clerk's Office of the District Court of the United States for the Southern District of New-York.

JOHN A. GRAY,
PRINTER & STEREOTYPER,
16 and 18 Jacob St.

PREFACE.

This book scarcely needs a preface. In my trip, I have kept my eyes and ears open, and have recorded all I have seen, heard and thought, which, it has appeared to me, would interest the community, or would throw light upon that question which now agitates our country from the Atlantic to the Pacific, and from the Saint Lawrence to the Gulf. I am an American citizen, and it is my prerogative to speak frankly and freely. I love our country, our *whole* country, and therefore I will not allow any earnestness of utterance to interfere with the spirit of conciliation and kindness.

JOHN S. C. ABBOTT.

FARMINGTON, MAINE.

SOUTH AND NORTH.

CHAPTER I.

THE VOYAGE.

Thursday, Dec. 1, 1859.—The steamer De Soto, on her regular trip, should have sailed at three o'clock, yesterday P.M., for New-Orleans *via* Havana; but, in consequence of some necessary repairs in the machinery, we were delayed a day. As the advertised hour was three o'clock, we took a carriage at one o'clock P.M., that we might avoid the great crowd ever assembling at the departure of one of these ocean steam-ships. At half-past one we reached the dock. The throng was already immense, and it took a long time before we could worm our way through the mass of carriages, carts, horses, men and piles of freight which encumbered the wharf.

At length the carriage arrived at the foot of the stairs, by which we were to ascend the side of the ship. The deck of the steamer was about as high above the wharf as the eaves of an ordinary two-story house; and an incessant crowd was passing up and down. We threaded our way through the multitude to seats at the stern of the ship, and sat down to contemplate the scene which, however familiar, is always interesting. The ship was crowded to its utmost capacity, with passengers and their friends, while two opposing currents were flowing incessantly in and out. A steam-engine was at work, raising immense piles of freight, a dozen boxes at a time, and lowering them into the capacious hold. The trunks also, similarly grouped, were rising high into the air and then sinking to unknown depths below. At the same time scores of men were at work upon the paddle-wheels and the engine, hammering with a deafening noise.

The whole aspect of the ship and of the wharf was that of chaotic uproar and confusion; for there were other ships and steamers all around in the closest possible proximity: some coming, some going, some getting up steam, some letting it off; while the whole harbor was alive with sailing vessels of every rig, and steamers of every pattern and size, in numbers which I in vain endeavored to count. Hour after hour thus passed away, and we seemed to be approaching no nearer the end of noise and confusion. The sun went down; darkness and the stars came, and lamps were lighted. Every ship in the harbor had lanterns in the shrouds; the streets of New-York were in a blaze of illumination. The opposite shores of Jersey City, Hoboken, and, far down the harbor, the hights of Staten Island, glittered like terrestrial constellations, actually out-rivaling the celestial clusters which the bright moon paled.

At seven o'clock, the ship still moored to the wharf, we were summoned to tea. Capacious as were the accommodations of the ship, it was soon evident that there were many more passengers than could be seated at the tables. It was found necessary to spread them twice, though there were two tables extending along the dining-saloon, about fifty feet in length.

At ten o'clock, the steamer left the wharf. The night was calm and brilliant, and the light of a waxing moon illumined the harbor. The sail down the bay and out of the narrows, the canopy above twinkling with stars, and the expanse below still more brilliant with the myriads of gas lights beaming from Long Island, Staten Island, Manhattan and the Jersey shore, presented a scene which wakes up the responses of the soul. It is now twelve o'clock at night. The land has entirely disappeared. A few light-houses glimmer in the distance with their intermittent or party-colored rays, and nothing else is to be seen but the sky above and the ocean around. Every state-room is filled, and the floor of the cabin is covered with sleepers upon mattresses. I have a pleasant room on deck, which is usually the smoking-room. It is about twelve feet square, and in consequence of the crowd of passengers, is fitted up with temporary berths. I share this room with nine young gentlemen, most of whom are Spaniards returning to Cuba after spending the summer at the North.

Friday, Dec. 2.—Last night the wind freshened, and we have to-day what the sailors would call a fine ten-knot breeze. The sun is bright, and the air fresh and mild. Though far from rough, our ship rises and falls over the ocean-swell sufficiently to make almost every passenger sick. We have one hundred and eighty passengers on board, and the various employés of the ship, consisting of sailors, waiters, firemen, engineers, etc., amount to one hundred more. Thus our little floating mansion, perhaps one hundred and thirty feet long by thirty feet wide, carries two hundred and eighty souls. At breakfast this morning, not more than twenty gentlemen were present, and but two ladies. One of these ladies sat for a moment, then, as the ship bowed gracefully over one of the waves, she turned ashy pale, and, with a tottering step, sought her state-room. It is hardly too much to say that the ship has this day presented but an aspect of misery. Pale, forlorn, woe-stricken faces meet you every where. Happy are they who can conceal themselves in state-rooms! Some are pillowed on the floor, some are seemingly dying upon the deck, occasionally uttering most pathetic groans, and hurrying with reeling footsteps to the sides of the ship. There is not a smile to be seen. The change is marvelous from the gayety and mirthfulness of yesterday to the gloom of to-day. A gentleman in condoling tones inquired of a lady how she felt.

"<u>Ah</u>!" said she, looking up languidly, "is that you? I have sounded to-day the very lowest depths of human misery!"

But sea-sickness, direful as is the woe, is one of those woes which only provoke the merriment of those who are not suffering from it. The aspect of our ship to-day would convince any one that "traveling is one of the most painful of pleasures." There are many children on board, screaming with discomfort, while their mothers and nurses are so sick that they can with difficulty hold up their heads.

About noon we plunged into a fog-bank, so dense that we could not see the length of the ship. Though all day long we had not seen a sail, occasionally, while groping through this fog-bank, the whistle was blown and the bell rung as a safe-guard against collision. We have been steaming along the coasts of Maryland and Virginia about one hundred miles from the shore. Night at length darkened gloomily around us. The decks were wet and slippery; the cabins suffocatingly close, and wailing of children, and still more painful utterances of sick passengers, fell every where upon the ear. There were few on board who did not earnestly wish that they were at home. And yet this was at the close of a day of unusually fine weather.

Saturday, Dec. 3.—The change is marvelous! In the night the wind died down to almost a perfect calm. The sun rose from the mirrored sea this morning with brilliance which can not be described. We are in the Gulf-stream, and it is a warm, balmy summer's day. Two or three sails are visible in the horizon. A school of black-fish amused us for a time with their gambols. Early in the morning an awning was spread over the decks to protect us from the sun. Nearly all have recovered from their sickness, for the noble De Soto glides along as smoothly as if we were in a river.

One can hardly imagine a more attractive scene than the decks now present. Groups of gentlemen and ladies, full of joy, leave not a space unoccupied. Children, attended by their slave nurses, who are black as ebony, and rotund in the most approved fashion of crinoline, are playing with their dolls. These young nurses are pretty girls "carved in ebony." They are probably selected for their good looks, as a gentleman loves to ride a handsome horse, and, being petted with light work and kind treatment and being as well fed, and about as well clothed as are their mistresses, they look contented and happy. They evidently love the children and the children love them. Their lot, *thus viewed*, certainly does not appear a hard one.

These Spanish children are, many of them, very fairy-like and beautiful, and they run around the deck with gentleness and politeness which seems instinctive to the race. I have never before seen a set of passengers on shipboard so truly refined. I have not yet heard an oath or witnessed an ungentlemanly act. Not even a pack of cards has been seen, and there has not been the slightest approach to intemperance. The spirit of rowdyism, so far as my observation extends, is almost peculiar to Young America. There are nine young Spanish gentlemen who occupy the room with me. We have to be very accommodating in dressing, as but two can dress at a time. But there has been, thus far, the constant exhibition of as much refinement and delicacy in word and action as the most scrupulous person could desire. This morning, in speaking of the very gentlemanly character of our companions, to one of our fellow-passengers, a gentleman of remarkable intelligence, and who has spent his life as a traveler, he remarked:

"Ah! if you wish to see the difference, you must go on board a ship of returning Californians. I have had my cheeks tingle with shame, when traveling with foreign gentlemen in my own country. There is no vulgar rowdyism in the world to be compared with that of young Americans."

It is a lamentable fact that there is a portion of our population, and a portion which esteems itself as belonging to the class of gentlemen, which seems to think that happiness can only be found in noise, coarseness and destruction. To them having a good time is to get half intoxicated, and to make night hideous with revelry.

All the day long we have glided over a smooth summer sea. One of the greatest pleasures of traveling consists in the number of very agreeable companions one makes. We have found on board this ship gentlemen and ladies of the most attractive character, with minds highly cultivated and manners polished by extended intercourse with the world. As we were sitting beneath the awning upon the deck to-day, fanned by a balmy breeze, with the decks crowded with peaceful and happy groups of gentlemen, ladies, and pleasant children, I turned to J. and said: ".This is truly *delicious*." Conscious that the epithet was not exactly appropriate, I could not be contented with one less expressive. But she promptly replied: "Yes, indeed, it is perfectly delicious."

By observation to-day at noon we were in latitude 35°, 13', that is, a little south of Cape Hatteras. For some unknown cause, storms seem to cluster around these perilous shoals which shoot far out from the Cape to the very edge of the Gulf-stream. Thousands of seamen have here found a watery grave. The current of the Gulf and the prevailing north-east winds drive the fog-enveloped ship upon the shoals, and there is no longer hope. We have had wonderfully pleasant weather in doubling the Cape. The Gulf-stream here is about one hundred miles broad, the temperature of the water being at 76°, and we have been nearly all day crossing this " river in the sea."

As the sun went down to-night, the moon came out from the clouds, and shone with great but intermittent brilliance. We sat upon the silent deck until a late hour enjoying the novel scene. There was not the slightest chill in the air, and it was a luxury to breathe. The whole day has been one of rare enjoyment. If traveling is sometimes the most painful of pleasures, it is also at other times the most delightful.

CHAPTER II.

TROPICAL SEAS.

Sabbath, Dec. 4.—Another delightful day. The sun rose brilliantly. A few fleecy clouds add to the beauty of the sky. A gentle southern breeze ripples the ocean without causing any breaking of the waves. Our ship's company, in quietude and external decorum, are as observant of the Sabbath as if all were devout Christians. We have one aged Cuban planter on board, eighty-eight years of age, a man of vast wealth, his property being estimated at over two millions of dollars. His brother, a Mississippi planter, recently died, leaving a still greater property. His cotton crop was often six thousand bales, which at fifty dollars a bale, the average price, brings in an income of three hundred thousand dollars. The whole expense of working this property was $60,000 a year. Thus he received a net income of $240,000 per annum. Such is the argument which sustains Slavery.

I am now writing in the cabin, which is about ten feet high above the water. The windows are all open, and the wind breathes most gratefully through. Groups are all around me talking in Spanish; some walking up and down the floor, some reclining on lounges and reading. The deck presents a still more animated spectacle. On the fore-deck, where the awning has not yet been spread, it is almost insupportably hot; on the spacious after-deck, beneath the awning, it is cool and delightful. Perhaps one hundred persons are assembled there, in such groups as elective affinities associate. The sun is bright, the ocean smooth, and we are in the rich enjoyment of a Sabbath which is the "bridal of the earth and sky."

Twelve o'clock at night.—This evening has been one such as is seldom enjoyed in a life-time.

Some one has said: "I would go farther to see a man than a mountain." We have had this evening both the *man* and the *mountain;* that is, the beauties of nature, and the joys of intellectual converse. As the sun sank beneath the waves, almost immediately, without any apparent transition of twilight, we were enveloped in the glories of one of the most brilliant of nights. The moon was in the zenith. Jupiter was beaming with its peculiarly mild lustre in the north-east; and those familiar constellations, which all have learned to love, the Pleiades, the Hyades and Orion, emerged one after another, seemingly from the bosom of the deep; while Sirius and Aldebaran, in rivalry strove to outshine each other. There was not the slightest chill in the air, and the deck was filled with groups of gentlemen and ladies, in quiet social converse, luxuriating in the scene.

The chief joy of traveling is, with me, the excitement of emotions which can be felt, but not described. The enjoyments of this evening were of that character. Our captain is an exceedingly agreeable man of high intellectual culture. We have also made the acquaintance of another gentleman on board who, in extent of information, is not surpassed by any man I have ever known. He is alike at home in science, in the classics and in all polite literature. He is familiar with all parts of the world, and is also a polished genntleman, and, that which is above all the rest, a genial Christian. Speaking half a dozen languages with as much fluency as if they were his mother tongue, and possessing a memory marvelously retentive of all he has seen and heard, he is one of the most agreeable companions that can be imagined.

We formed a little social group this evening, five of us, consisting of the captain, our friend Mr. C., a highly accomplished and well-informed lady, J. and myself; and hour after hour glided away in the most delightful social communion. No book that was ever penned has contained so charming a variety. There was mirth and pensiveness, sublimity and comicality, profound philosophy and the play of fancy, history, biography, anecdote, tears and smiles, and all this while gliding along over a tropical sea, and beneath a serene sky, illumined by moon and stars. One does not enjoy many such evenings in a life-time. The midnight chime of eight bells was struck before I left the deck.

Monday morning, Dec. 5.—We have had a sultry night, but the sea was smooth, the wind fair, and we have been gliding on our way at the rate of eleven miles an hour. This morning I arose with the sun. The sky was cloudless, and though the fresh trade wind scarcely broke a wave upon the ocean, our ship rose and fell majestically over those strange billows which sailors call a ground swell, and which poets have spoken of as the heaving of ocean's bosom while she sleeps.

The arrangement for meals on ship-board, is breakfast, informally from a quarter of eight to nine; lunch at twelve; dinner, two tables, in consequence of the great number of passengers, first table from one to two, second from two to three; supper at seven.

At an early hour this bright morning, the awnings were spread, and the passengers crowded upon deck. All the windows of the cabins were thrown open, and what are called windsails were arranged to carry a current of fresh air through the heated rooms. It is now eleven o'clock, and quite oppressively warm. I have left the crowd sitting beneath the awnings on the deck, and with no little self-denial have come down into the cabin to add to my journal. Seated in a chair, which is a fixture, I am writing at one of the marble tables, which also can not be moved. Several little children are playing around upon the floor, talking Spanish, and many gentlemen and ladies are seated around the spacious saloon, some reading, and others conversing. Through the state-room windows, when the doors are left open, I can see the sky, so bright and clear, and occasionally catch a glimpse of a sparkling wave, as our ship plunges through it.

This morning as I was sitting upon the deck, a very benignant looking gentleman, apparently about sixty years of age, came and took a seat by my side. I found him to be a Cuban planter, gentlemanly, frank, and peculiarly kind in his feelings. We talked for an hour, and I can only regret that I can not record every word which he said, just as it was uttered; for in such a record there could not be the slightest violation of propriety. I can only give the substance.

He said, that for a respectable plantation in Cuba, one needed two thousand acres of land, and two hundred negroes. That the laborers would average about ten hogsheads of sugar each, bringing a net profit of four hundred dollars, and that thus the net profits of the plantation would be $80,000. This he considered pretty fair business. An able-bodied slave would readily bring 1500 dollars, and the planters generally preferred those freshly imported from Africa to those who were natives of Cuba, because the newly arrived Africans have *less vices*. He did not seem to think slavery efficient as a *missionary institution*. As a general rule, all the inhabitants of the Island, with the exception of the authorities, were in favor of the slave-trade, as they were anxious to get as many negroes as possible, but that he did not think it right to tear the poor creatures from their homes in Africa, and that he had just been arguing the point with a brother planter on board.

There were, he said, many of what are called "poor whites" upon the Island, but that there was no suffering from poverty; that the climate was so luxurious that but little clothing was needed, and that a small sweet-potato patch, and a few plantain trees would give one of these families all they wanted. "We have," said he, "no winter with us, as you have, to pinch up those people and make them work. It is often said," he continued, "that if the Island were to fall into the hands of the French, or the English, or the Americans, they would soon make things look differently. But I have observed that whoever comes to our tropical climate, feels its enervating effects, and soon becomes as indolent as any of us."

This man's nature seemed to overflow with kindness. I am sure that neither horse, nor cow, nor slave would intentionally be treated with any cruelty by him. But there is another planter on board, whose property is estimated by millions, who looks to me like a hard man. The domestic slaves on board, who are the waiting maids of the matrons and young ladies, appear petted and happy; but there is one poor girl here, black as jet, who looks forlorn enough.

A gentleman told an anecdote yesterday, of Andrew Jackson, which was new to me, and quite illustrative of that frank, blunt man. The General once invited a clergyman, for whom he had a high regard, to dine with him. One of the officers, an infidel, rudely assailed the clergyman with the question: "Do you really believe, sir, that there is such a place as hell?" General Jackson instantly interposed in a strong voice, which arrested the attention of the whole company.

"I, sir, believe there is such a place as hell!"

"Indeed, sir," said the officer, "and may I inquire on what ground you found your belief?"

"Because," the General replied, "if there were no hell, there would be no appropriate place in the future world for such persons as you are."

And this led to an equally characteristic anecdote respecting George Washington. He one day invited several of his staff to dine with him. In the course of the dinner, one of the officers uttered an oath. Washington struck the table with his knife, producing instant silence, and then said in a low, sad voice: "I thought I had invited none but gentlemen to dine with me to-day."

There are sad scenes on board; invalids pale and weak, seeking a southern clime, hoping for health, but doubtless to die. In the pleasant afternoons they come upon deck, look pensively upon the gay throng, try to smile, but oh! what sadness in a smile which can not veil a sorrow-stricken heart. As it breezes up a little, they draw their shawls around them; the hectic flush, the hollow cough, reveals their doom to all but to themselves. At an early hour they go down to the solitude, the silence of their state-rooms. God is there with them. He sees their tears and hears their prayers. "May you die at home," is an eastern benediction.

There is one young mother here. She has left two babes at home with her husband, and has with her two lovely children, a son and a daughter of six and four. She is going to Cuba to pass the winter; poor mother! summers and winters will come and go, but she may never see her New-York home again. She says that nothing could have induced her to leave her babes but love for them; that she must do every thing in her power, for their sakes, to prolong her life. Thus joy and sadness meet us. In contrast there is on board a beautiful Spanish bride, who can not have numbered more than seventeen summers. She is returning from her bridal-tour to the United States, and is full of health and joy. Her young husband is devoted to her; they have evidently wealth, and her buoyancy of spirits, fluency of speech, and lively repartees, surround her with an atmosphere of mirth.

I have had a long conversation to-day with a lady from St. Thomas, a small but commercially important Island, nearly a thousand miles east from Havana. This Island belongs to the Danish government, and contains six hundred thousand whites, and the same number of blacks. About twelve years ago, these blacks, then slaves, were all emancipated by the home government. The white inhabitants were all opposed to this act at the time, but she thinks that they would not now wish to have slavery reëstablished. She gave me almost precisely the same account of the poor blacks in St. Thomas, which the Cuban planter gave me of the poor whites in Cuba. The climate is so genial, and sweet potatoes and fruit so abundant, that people can live in semi-barbaric comfort, almost without labor. There is, however, this difference, the poor whites in Cuba can not be induced to work for wages, but there is no difficulty in hiring the services of the blacks.

She says that the blacks are all perfectly submissive to law, that there is the kindest state of feeling between them and the whites, and that the idea of any danger from them, on account of lawlessness or insurrection, never occurs to any mind. The Island is very small, with no large plantations. Energetic white men spend a few years there in trade, until they accumulate a comfortable fortune, and then move to some place where they can enjoy it. The blacks having no strong motive for work, are a harmless, indolent, untroubled people, religiously inclined, slumbering their years away in a state of great contentment.

Our voyage is so delightful that I am looking forward with regret to its close. This afternoon and evening the whole ship's company seemed to be assembled upon the decks. Though a hundred miles out at sea, we were coasting along the banks of the most majestic and extraordinary river upon the globe.

"There is a river," says M. F. Maury, "in the ocean. In the severest droughts it never fails, and in the mightiest floods it never overflows. Its banks and its bottoms are of cold water, while its surface is of warm. The Gulf of Mexico is its fountain, and its mouth is in the Arctic Seas. It is the Gulf-Stream. There is in the world no other such majestic flow of waters. Its current is more rapid than the Mississipi or the Amazon, and its volume more than a thousand times greater.

"Its waters, as far out from the Gulf as the Carolina coasts, are of an indigo blue. They are so distinctly marked, that their line of junction with the common sea-water, may be traced by the eye. Often one half of the vessel may be seen floating in the Gulf-Stream water, while the other half is in common water of the sea."

We have crossed this magnificent stream where it was about one hundred miles in breadth, and are now coasting down its eastern shores, that we may avoid the flow of its central current. The deep ultra-marine of the pelagic river, stands in marked contrast with the almost prairie-green of the ocean through which this mysterious flood is poured.

All have seemed reluctant, this balmy night, to retire to the hot cabins. The moon is nearly full, and the most gorgeous of the constellations look down upon us from these tropic skies. We expect to make the light upon Great Isaacs, a vast rock emerging from the great Bahama banks, at twelve o'clock at night. As this will be the first land we make since leaving New-York, I am anxious to see it, and, if possible, in the bright moonlight, to catch a view of the long line of rocks, the tops of oceanic mountains, which we skirt for many leagues. I therefore now "turn in," to be called up at twelve o'clock.

Tuesday morning, Dec. 6.—We have another bright and sunny day. The trade winds blowing freshly from the north-east, fill our sails, and the steamer rises over and plunges through the waves gloriously, with the speed of a race-horse, dashing the billows in broad furrows of foam from her bows. It is half-past ten o'clock A.M. The canvas awning covers the spacious after-deck, and more than a hundred persons are clustered beneath it. We have three nuns on board, sisters of the Sacred Heart, in their antique ungainly costume. Two of them are young and pretty, and evidently as vain of their accoutrements as ever was city belle of her Parisian trousseau. They are very plump, and in such good condition of rubicund cheek and embonpoint, as to prove that neither vigils nor penance are hard upon the flesh. The fare of the anchorite must certainly be very nutritious. A lady of our party, who has been to Rome, seen the Pope, and touched, though not kissed the brazen toe, quite won the heart of one of these sisters by her narrative. "But I should think," said the lady to the pretty little nun, "it would be very hard for you to do the very toilsome work of the nunnery."

"I assure you, madam," said the sister, twirling her prayer-book, and with a pout which would have honored any drawing-room in Fifth Avenue, "that these hands never did any other work than to decorate the altar."

"Are you sisters of charity!" asked the lady very innocently.

"Sisters of charity!" she replied, "no!" and then, as if worldly ambition was becoming too triumphant, she said: "I am afraid I am not good enough to be a sister of charity, they have so much to suffer and to do." Having done this penance, the young heart, true to its frail instincts, revealed itself in the words: "We are Ladies of the Sacred Heart! We belong to the Society of Jesus! We are the *highest order* in the Church!"

Alas! for poor human nature. The pride of aristocratic rank throbs in the bosom of the hooded nun as warmly as it flows beneath the diadem and the coronet. How beautiful is the religion of Jesus, overreaching all forms and all creeds. "God is a spirit, and they that worship him must worship him in spirit and in truth." There is much in the appearance of these simple-hearted girls to interest one.

They are young, enthusiastic, and apparently sincere. They have their share of the ordinary frailties of humanity. But how kind the declaration: "Like as a father pitieth his children, so the Lord pitieth them that fear him, for he knoweth our frame, he remembereth that we are dust." I can not look upon their artless, benevolent, though complacent faces, without feeling that they are disciples of the Saviour, groping their way, perhaps as directly as many others of less artificial faith, towards heaven.

Very prettily one of them said this morning: "I do so pity the *world's people* on board, they look so troubled and care-worn. I pray for them all the time. But we, in the nunnery, have nothing but peace and joy, and escape from all temptations."

The lady was too keen-sighted not to see her opportunity, and with softness which the nun herself could not surpass, rejoined: "But some must perform life's toils, and triumph over life's temptations; and is it quite right for us to escape from these duties, that we may find a more easy path to heaven?"

This broadside was so sudden and unlooked for, that our inexperienced nun, for a moment, was quite staggered; and rather ungraciously she beat a retreat, exclaiming, with no little pique: "Ah! madam, you are very much mistaken if you suppose there are no trials and sacrifices to be encountered in the nunnery."

Some one expressed surprise that they were permitted to converse so freely with the people of the world on board. But they replied that they had from their ecclesiastical superiors, a special dispensation to that end, during the voyage. It was evidently to their youthful hearts quite a spiritual oasis in the desert of their ecclesiasticism. Like birds from the cage, they enjoyed their hour of liberty to the utmost.

As I am now writing on the deck, with my tablet in my lap, these worthy girls are sitting at my side, looking very devotional, and reading their prayer-books. Probably they are not aware of the spirit of ostentation which may secretly mingle with the holiest purposes of their hearts. If God accepts no homage but that which is *perfectly* pure, alas for man! But "He knoweth our frame." May God hear the prayers of these simple nuns, and bear them in his loving arms to heaven.

By my side there is another group. The prominent figures are two African nurses, Cuban slaves of Ethopia's darkest hue. They each have a beautiful white child, of about two years of age, in their arms. A young gentleman and lady are talking and laughing with them, very pleasantly, without the slightest recognition of any difference in color. Indeed, it is by no means improbable that both of them have nestled in the bosom of these ebon nurses, drawing from these breasts their nourishment. The love of the nurses for the children is manifestly hearty and sincere. Such honest smiles and caressings can not be assumed. One of these beautiful infant children pats the cheek of her nurse, now one cheek, and now the other, and now, placing a hand on each cheek, she presses her little ruby lip to the thick, dark lips of her laughing attendant, and kisses her again and again, as lovingly as ever a child embraced a mother.

My observation has ever taught me that the African race is peculiarly loving in its nature. We had a colored nurse for one of our children, and that nurse still loves that child as if she were her own. Many who only see such a phase of Slavery as is exhibited by the most favored household servants, in the kindest families, have no conception whatever of what Slavery is, on the distant plantations, consigning millions to a state of heathenism.

CHAPTER III.

CUBA.

Tuesday, Dec. 6.—At a little past twelve o'clock this morning, Captain B. very kindly came to my berth, which is on deck in a room almost adjoining his office, and informed me that we had just made the light-house on the Great Isaac. We had crossed the Matenilla reef, and passed the western point of the Great Bahama, without seeing it, as it was night, though the distance was not such but that we might have seen it by day. The revolving light, on a rock just emerging from the sea, shone with a long golden gleam over the mirrored water, and the stars glittered in these clear tropical skies with a brilliance which I have never seen surpassed. For two hours we paced the deck, and they were hours of rich enjoyment.

The whole day has been one of the most lovely that ever dawned upon the tropics, and it has passed like a dream of beauty and joy. The deck was crowded with happy faces; the sea was smooth and bright and sparkling; we passed several ships under full sail, and were interested in watching the innumerable keys or mounds of rock, emerging from the sea, by which we were rapidly gliding.

About five o'clock in the afternoon we caught a glimpse of the hills of Cuba, in the vicinity of Matanzas. But darkness came before we arrived near enough to the land to discern objects on the shore.

Wednesday, Dec. 7.—The night has been sultry—oppressively so. I found it difficult to sleep even with the door and windows of our cabin open. I rose at four o'clock in the morning and went upon deck. There in the bright moonlight, at hardly a stone's cast from our steamer, lay the island Cuba, the queen of the Antilles. A light-house, shining with a very brilliant light, rose from the frowning towers and bastions of the Moro Castle at the entrance of the harbor, and the city of Havana slumbered in the silence of the undawned morning.

We had reached the mouth of the beautiful harbor about one o'clock, and for five hours were compelled to "lay off and on," as the sailors phrase it, the laws of the island not allowing any ship to enter the harbor between sun-set and sun-rise. At six o'clock, just as the sun was rising over the ramparts of the Cabana, the De Soto gracefully entered the narrow passage, and passing between the guns of the Moro and the Punta, glided to the centre of the harbor, which is one of the most spacious and beautiful in the world, and cast anchor about a mile from the shore.

The scene which now opened itself to an eye, hitherto all unused to tropical scenery and tropical vegetation, can not be described. The harbor was filled with vessels of every kind, and the flags of all nations drooped at their mast-heads. Bugles were pealing from the ships of war, whose vast hulks lay motionless as islands upon the still waters of the bay, and from the fortresses, so massive, frowning upon the shore. Not a breath of air was moving; not a cloud was in the sky, and the sun shone down upon the green surrounding hills, waving with orange groves, cocoas, and palms, upon the red tiles of the city, and upon the unrippled water, with an intensity of heat which I have never known equalled at that early hour.

Immediately upon our casting anchor, boats, in large numbers, pushed out from the small, low wharves, or landing places of the city; all with awnings over their sterns, and nearly all with masts, and sails ready to be unfurled should any breath of wind arise. These boats, in structure, very much resemble the Venetian gondola, only more clumsy in their build, and the awnings were of coarse, soiled canvas without any gracefulness of drapery or picturesqueness of color. I counted thirty of these boats, at one time, approaching our ship, and was surprised to find that the rowers were almost invariably white men. I afterwards learned that it is more profitable to employ the slaves on the plantations than in the city, and that it is deemed prudent to keep them separated as much as possible from white laborers. An incautious sailor might utter words of freedom which would excite troublesome thoughts in the bondman's breast.

The stairs were let down the ship's side, and soon there was a large fleet waiting to convey those who might wish to disembark to the shore. But no one could leave until the government officials should come on board and grant us permission; and those dignitaries, being in no haste to cut short their breakfasts, kept us waiting an hour. But while thus waiting there was among the boatmen no noise, no oaths, no contention, but on the contrary much apparent gentleness and politeness. At length a beautiful boat was seen approaching, with rich decorations, beneath which were shaded on soft cushions the government officers. These gentlemen ascended the sides of our ship, examined the papers, pronounced all right, and we were permitted to land.

The captain of the De Soto informed us that he should remain at anchor until two o'clock in the afternoon, when the ship would continue her voyage to New-Orleans. We had thus six hours in which to visit the city.

At eight o'clock we took one of these barges for the shore, and seating ourselves beneath the shade of the awning, rapidly were rowed along among the shipping to the governmental pier, where the licensed boatman was compelled first to carry us, that we might pay one dollar each for permission to visit the island. The boatman's fare was fifty cents each. We were so fortunate as to find in the boat with us, I having three ladies under my charge, a gentleman, resident in Havana, who spoke English perfectly. He kindly aided, when we arrived at the custom-house landing, in obtaining our permits, and called two *volantes*, the peculiar cab of the country, to take us to "Dominico's," where we expected to get some refreshments.

All are familiar with descriptions of these volantes. They are very comical vehicles, and few persons ever get into them for the first time without a hearty laugh. The established fare is twenty cents for any distance within a mile. We had been told that the drivers would always impose upon foreigners if they could. We rode through the narrow paved streets, between stone houses of the most antique and primitive architecture, for about one eighth of a mile, until we arrived at Dominico's, a perfect specimen of a huge, stone-floored, Moorish inn. When I offered the negro drivers the fare, they both remonstrated, refusing to take it, and jabbered away most volubly in Spanish, not one word of which could we understand.

Not wishing to be imposed upon, I looked around and seeing a very intelligent-looking gentleman passing by, I addressed him, inquiring if he spoke English.

"Non, monsieur," he replied, "je suis Français."

I then told him, in French, of my difficulty,

and asked if I had offered the proper fare. He assured me that I had, and turning to the negroes denounced them severely for their intended fraud. Thanking him for his kindness and dropping the fare into the hands of the negroes, we entered the restaurant.

It was a large room, on a level with the street, paved almost like the street, with a spacious bar glittering with decanters, and with marble tables around. The entrance-door was very large, so that the room seemed almost a part of the street. There were two very pleasant-looking young gentlemen there, and, I hardly know how, we almost instantly became acquainted with them, found that they were from New-York, and that they were acquainted with our names, exchanged cards and received from them the most extraordinary acts of kindness. They informed us what refreshments to call for, and then informed us that the bill was paid; conducted us to several very interesting places in the immediate vicinity, and took leave of us, as the barouche, according to appointment, arrived at the door. Such attentions to strangers in a strange land were, of course, very gratifying.

We had engaged a very intelligent driver who spoke English. He drove us through the principal streets of the queer, antique, Spanish city; took us to the grand cathedral; to the tomb of Christopher Columbus; to the Bishop's Garden, once the pride of the island, now going to decay; to the palace of the governor, whose title is Captain General; to the palaces of several Spanish nobles, and out into the country, where we were regaled with the bloom of flowers we had never before seen, and the luxuriance of tropical vegetation which rose like an oriental vision upon our eyes. Palm trees, cocoas, bananas, and orange trees laden with their golden fruit, every where met the view. At the fruiterer's stalls we almost filled our barouche with fruit—five large, rich, sweet oranges for five cents; cocoa-nuts, full of their cool, refreshing milk, which we drank luxuriously from the shell, at the same price; rich bunches of bananas for ten cents. We shall never forget this day. Though all say that one soon wearies of Havana, we found so much to interest us, so much of entire novelty, that we regretted very much that we could not remain a few days longer.

Some scenes we witnessed which were excessively revolting. The blacks, bare-headed and bare-legged, with countenances less expressive than many a brute, seemed sunk to the very lowest state of human debasement. Many of them had almost lost the aspect of humanity. Negro girls of seventeen or eighteen, that age usually so interesting, sauntered through the streets in rags and dirt, with one single robe, which seemed never to have entered the wash-tub, partially covering the person, exciting the deepest emotion of disgust mingled with compassion.

But the object most revolting, and which continues to haunt my mind, and I think will till I die, was the aspect of the Coolies. It seemed to me that human misery could sink no lower. Their doom is vastly worse than that of the slaves. These wretched Chinese are lured to leave their country, as we were informed, with the promise that, for their services for eight years, they should be taken, without expense, to Cuba, be fed and clothed, and receive four dollars a month. Thus at the end of eight years, they would have three hundred and eighty-four dollars. This seems like an immense sum to a poor Chinaman, to whom a cent a day is a very respectable competence. Thousands are thus induced to embark. None, probably, return. They are sold upon their arrival for about four hundred dollars. If the owner can wear them out in eight years, so that they die, he of course has nothing to pay. If he can not, he sends them to some distant plantation, or sells them again to some one who still claims eight years' service. They are ignorant, debased, and powerless. There is no one to plead their cause, and their doom is sealed. I know not what the sins of Sodom were, but it is safe to say that there could be nothiug there exceeding this iniquity.

As no females are brought, only young men aud boys, these poor wretches can have no home and no family ties. Two hundred thousand of them, it is said, have been imported to Cuba within the last seven years. These are all Chinese. A likely negro will bring fifteen hundred dollars. But these Coolies will bring but four hundred, for though it is generally supposed that there will be no end to their slavery, the purchaser nominally buys merely the privilege of employing them for eight years at four dollars a month. The poor creatures seem soon to awake to a sense of their helpless and hopeless condition. Many of them commit suicide; and many in despair sicken and die.

It is said, with how much truth I do not know, that the East-India Coolies, taken to the British Islands, have their rights carefully protected by the British government. The contracts are carefully drawn up; the Coolies are placed under the shelter of the laws, and the provisions of the contract are firmly enforced. The arrangement in itself would be eminently a wise one, if conducted with justice and humanity. There is a vast over-supply of labor in the crowded East-Indies, and a great want of labor in the sparsely populated West-Indies. The terms offered are fair, and the bargain, if honestly enforced, is advantageous to both parties. But I find it to be the universal impression that in Cuba the Coolie trade is merely a Chinese slave-trade under the most fraudulent and cruel circumstances.

Seeing a group of several hundred of these wretched Coolies, working in the blazing sun upon a road, I requested our driver to take us through them all. Such a spectacle of misery I never saw, or conceived of before! Nearly all of them were naked to the waist. They were excessively filthy in person, and their countenances of the most abject debasement and joylessness. Several overseers, with limber whips in their hands, were standing beneath the shade of trees, watching them and directing their work. It is said, however, to be unsafe to whip them. Their religion inculcates such ideas of the dignity of the human body, that the degradation of a blow can only be atoned for by the death of him who strikes it, or by the self-martyrdom of him who has received it. If a Coolie is whipped, somebody must die.

The mind is appalled by the contemplation of these miseries. What is to be the doom of these debased and fallen races? How are they to be rescued from the tyranny of pride and avarice, and elevated to the dignity of manhood? They need the tenderest care and the most self-denying toils of their more favored brothers, to raise them, from the gulf into which they have fallen, to that rank which all should attain, who were originally created "but a little lower than the angels." And yet their wiser and more powerful brothers exhaust their shrewdness and energy in endeavors to rivet their chains and to plunge them still deeper in the abyss.

Cuba, as God made it, with its hills and vales, its flowers, groves, bird-songs, its fruits and sunny skies, and verdure and salubrious clime, is indeed the gem of the ocean. God formed it apparently for a terrestrial paradise. But man has made it the most corrupt and joyless spot in the expanse of Christendom. It is the universal declaration that bribery and corruption are the fundamental principles of the government. There is no civil liberty, and no religious toleration. Church and State are alike debased into mere engines of despotism.

The annexation of Cuba to the United States, were it possible, while it would strengthen slavery in the Senate and in the House, would in many respects greatly weaken the institution in the continental states. It would be the instant destruction of every sugar plantation in Louisiana. Not one could live a year. This island is eight hundred miles in length, and from twenty-five to a hundred and thirty in breadth, and contains forty-three thousand three hundred and eighty square miles. Its whole population is about a million, nearly two thirds of whom are slaves or free blacks. In fertility of soil and adaptation to the culture of sugar, the island is unequaled, and yet millions of acres are yet unoccupied, it being estimated that not seven per cent of the whole island is at present brought under cultivation. Annexation, removing the heavy duty now imposed upon Cuban sugar, for the protection of the Louisiana planter, would instantly break up every sugar plantation in the States. But I understand that many of the Louisiana planters do not object to this. They would sell their plantations to cotton-growers. Two days' sail would take them and their negro gangs to Cuba. A few days' work would rear the negro huts; and, with the skill already acquired, and the machinery which could be easily moved, they would recommence operations on a scale far more favorable than ever before. On the hill sides and in the valleys of Cuba, many miles from the main land, there would be no chance for the slaves to escape, and no sounds from the free North could reach their ears, and no rays of light from the sun of liberty could penetrate their darkened eyes.

Under these circumstances we should probably see such a stampede of slaveholders, with their slaves, to Cuba, as the world has never seen before. The sugar plantations without exception would be abandoned. Carolinians and Georgians would forsake their worn-out fields, where "fanatics" annoy them, for this new, more inviting, and safer realm for the institution. Slaves would be in greater demand than ever before. The slave-breeders on the border States would sell off their stock with rapidity hitherto unparalleled, impelled by the double motive of increased price, and increased danger of escape by the "underground railroad." Thus the wave which is sweeping the black population down towards the Gulf of Mexico, would receive an impetus of wonderful power. None would go to Cuba but determined slaveholders. The continental States would be greatly drained. There would be an immense accumulation on the island; and then, alas! might come the catastrophe—the reënactment of the tragedy of St. Domingo! May God avert that awful hour.

It is barely *possible* that providences may be moving in that direction. Though there are great and obvious evils visible in the annexation of Cuba—strengthening, as it would, the vote of slavery, and bringing a people of foreign tongue and uncongenial habits and religion, to partake with us in the responsibilities of our government, while we are already sufficiently embarrassed with hostile and destructive influences, still it is manifest that such a measure would tend greatly to drain the Southern States of their slaves, and would facilitate, in the most wonderful manner, the emancipation of the border States from slave-breeding and slave labor. If we are doomed to the evil of this extension of American slavery, we must accept the results to which I have alluded as in part compensation; and we must solace ourselves with the faith, that,

> "God moves in a mysterious way
> His wonders to perform."

It would indeed be singular, if in this way the dark tide of Slavery were to be setting from our shores to a distant Island; that God, instead of leading Lot from Sodom, should take Sodom from Lot. God is even now moving with a power which no earthly contrivance can resist, in freeing Missouri, Kentucky, Maryland and Virginia from Slavery. It is as certain that they must soon be free, as that the snows of winter shall melt before the returning sun of spring. Other States will then become border-States, and will inevitably follow in the same course. The doom of Slavery is sealed. Move which way he may, the slaveholder loses the game.

But, on the other hand, I find no one who thinks it *possible* that Cuba can be annexed. There are but two conceivable measures of annexation, namely, *purchase* or *seizure*, and from both of these, it is the judgment of all with whom I converse, that we are excluded.

1. We can not purchase. Spain will not sell at any price. Castilian pride is up. We may just as well, so far as I could learn, attempt to buy the Spanish province of Grenada or Estremadura. Cuba is now deemed the brightest gem in the Spanish coronet. Spain is beginning to awake from the slumber of ages, and is reviving in wealth and power. Within a few years, Spain has constructed five thousand miles of railroad; and railroads are efficient teachers and powerful reformers. Light and vigor from the French Court are penetrating the peninsula. I have not yet conversed with a man who has thought that there was any more chance that Spain would sell Cuba, than that we would sell the District of Columbia. Suppose England were to vote a few millions for the purchase of Washington, thinking, that, as the Union is to be dissolved, and as the North and South may probably quarrel about the property at the

Capital, we may be willing to sell out. So far as I can learn, Spain regards our offers to purchase Cuba in the light in which we should regard such a proposition. She resents the movement as an insult. I know nothing about the secrets of Cabinets, but this seems to be the universal opinion as to the *purchase* of Cuba.

2. We can not *seize* the Island. England and France will not let us. This is understood to be an established fact. Young America is very plucky; but England, France, and Spain united, would make a troublesome foe. Our navy is not quite strong enough to blow those three navies out of the water. We shall not attempt it.

Besides, we should not be united among ourselves. There is a *conscience* at the North which says, *seize* means *steal;* an *opinion*, which declares that the motive would be the extension, consolidation, and perpetuation of Slavery. This the North dreads with all the power of what the South calls *fanaticism*, and the North *religion*. We can not seize Cuba. We can not buy. We shall continue to look wistfully at it. That is all.

It is said that the late Captain-General of the Island, Concha, returned to Spain with three millions of dollars, as his perquisites, collected during an administration of five years. All his vast group of retainers return with him, also proportionately rewarded. A new Captain-General, Sereno, and a new swarm from the Castilian Court, have just arrived, and are now busy filling their purses.

At 2 o'clock P.M., we returned to the ship. The steam was up, and the paddle-wheels revolving. In a few moments we were under weigh, and, gliding out of the beautiful harbor, between the frowning batteries of the Moro and the Punta, entered the open and mirrored sea. The sun is now sinking behind a bank of heavy clouds, ominous of a storm. The dim outline of the Island is still visible, and will soon be lost in the approaching darkness. Even as I pen these lines, the short tropical twilight has faded away, and it is night upon the sea. The mountains of Cuba are dissolved in the gloom, and my eyes will probably never rest upon them again. Cuba, farewell! Thou hast a dreadful account to render at the judgment day. Neither Chorazin nor Bethsaida need dread a heavier doom.

CHAPTER IV.

THE SLAVE'S CABIN, AND THE FREEMAN'S COTTAGE.

Thursday Dec. 8.—A stern *norther* rose in the night, blowing fiercely across the current of the Gulf, and raising that short, chopped sea, as the sailors term it, for which the English Channel is renowned, and which provokes the excess of sea discomfort. Nearly all on board were simply miserable. The gale shrieked through the rigging; dark masses of vapor shrouded the sky, and clouds of spray swept the decks. The ship rolled and plunged amidst these billows, every timber apparently creaking with the strain, and the only place of refuge was one's berth. I could neither read nor write, nor remain upon the wind-swept, wave-washed deck. The whole day has been dark and comfortless. Night is now around us. We are in the middle of the Gulf, and there is but little prospect of sleep. The suffering from sickness, of many on board, is very severe. Travel, surely, has its pains, as well as its pleasures.

Friday, Dec. 9.—A dismal night, and a dismal day. But few have ventured to the table. Ledges are attached to confine the plates, that they may not slide, as our ship plunges and rolls over the billows. The day has furnished no record, but the monotony of gloom and suffering. The wind, the clouds, the piercing chill, and the raging waves, have made our ship a prison, where not a joyous sight is seen, or a pleasant sound heard, and where many a groan falls upon the ear. These are the dark days of the voyager; days of real misery, but which are fortunately forgotten as soon as over.

Saturday, Dec. 10.—This day has been as bright, externally and internally, as the two preceding days have been black and woeful.

Last evening the wind abated, the clouds dispersed, and the full moon turned night almost into day. The Captain judged that we should make the light-house, at the mouth of the Mississippi, at twelve o'clock at night. As I was anxious to see the Balize where this wondrous river pours its turbid flood into the Gulf, and by its immense deposits, is creating leagues of land, I arose at twelve o'clock, and went upon the deck. There was the bright light at the entrance of one of the four arms of the river, beaming directly before us.

The norther, which had been blowing for forty-eight hours, had swept, apparently, every particle of moisture from the sky; and the full-orbed moon, which had just passed the zenith, shone effulgent, almost as a sun. Vast reaches of mud-banks were all around, through which, in pools, and channels, and lagoons, flowed the turbid flood of the Mississippi. A more dismal scene can hardly be imagined; and still it was a scene upon which the geologist must look with intensest interest.

From the immense water-shed of a valley, unsurpassed by that of any other on the globe, and from a distance of thousands of miles, this majestic stream, with energy which never tires, is bringing its accumulations, by millions of cart-loads daily, to fill up the Gulf of Mexico. We have but to wait long enough, that is, but a few millions of years, when we shall have the most admirable railroad plateau directly to Cuba. The work is going on surely, and without intermission. I hope that the awful tragedy of time and sin will be brought to a close long before those ages shall have rolled away.

There are four main channels of the river, branching off from a point about fourteen miles above the localities where these streams now enter the gulf. The whole of this region is a marsh of soft mud, here and there covered with a rank growth of coarse grass; the surface of the land, if it may so be called, being hardly perceptibly above that of the sea. Upon one of these mud-banks at the mouth, reared upon a foundation of piles driven into the ooze, there is a light-house, and a telegraph station, which, on the arrival of any ship, sends the tidings a hundred and ten miles up the river to New-Orleans. A few dredging-steamers were also slumbering upon the mud. We fired a gun, and screamed with all the strength of our brazen-throated engine, in the vain attempt to rouse the telegraph-operator. But we were quite unable to turn him out in the cold morning air, and the steamer renewing its speed, breasted the current of the stream, and pressed on.

For nearly fifty miles, I should think, from the mouth of the river, nothing is to be seen but the dismal marsh, land which the river has made, in recent ages, and so wet and spongy as to be quite unhabitable. These vast operations of nature, God's enginery, require ages for their consummation. At length we came to the more solid land where vegetation began to assume the luxuriance, bloom and verdure of a virgin world. The prairie has its beauty as well as the mountain, and to my eye the landscape soon assumed an aspect of marvelous loveliness. The plain extended, smooth as a floor, on each side of the river, to the forests of live oaks and cypress, which concealed and decorated the swamps in the rear. If we say that "distance lends enchantment to the view," it was truly "enchantment" which distance did lend.

The houses of the planters were generally plain, square, substantial mansions, surrounded with verandahs, embowered in groves of the ever-verdant orange and live oak, and presenting an aspect of much comfort. Some of these dwellings were of considerable architectural beauty, though I saw none which vied with the villas and palaces which opulence is rearing at the North.

At a little distance from the planter's mansion, were to be seen, almost invariably, in two parallel rows, the neat white-washed cabins of the negroes. We would generally count from ten, to forty or fifty. They looked, in the distance, very neat and very pretty. They were of one story, apparently contained but one room, seemed to be well guarded from the rain, and, very frequently, had either in front or rear, a projection of the roof, where the children could play, or the old people sit, protected from the sun. Some ladies at my side, said: "How pleasant these plantations look! How comfortably these servants are provided for! How can people say that the slaves are cruelly treated!" This is the South side view. I have endeavored to give it fairly.

But, in looking at this question, we must first settle a more important one, and that is, What is man? Is he under any circumstances a mere animal, formed only to toil like the horse or the ox, and then to pass away—or is he an immortal being, endowed with powers capable of endless expansion, and bound here to cultivate all his capabilities, moral, intellectual, and æsthetic, to the utmost? A horse is treated kindly when well stabled; a pig when well penned. But is a man treated kindly when well cabined? No! No! He is heaven-born. He has limitless faculties, he has an exalted nature to be developed and cultured. And any system which shuts him up to ignorance, which dwarfs his noblest nature, so that he can by no possibility attain the maturity of manhood, is cruelty in the extreme. Misfortune may curve the spine, or blind the eye, or wither the limb, and the well-developed soul shall move freely and joyously, and the world shall do it homage. But when the soul itself is palsied and imbruted, all its aspirations crushed, and all its celestial energies paralyzed, I can not receive the doctrine that the *man* is kindly treated, because the straw on which he sleeps is clean, and the roof which covers him is tight, and the corn he eats is nutritious.

I enter the cabin of the slave, and say earnestly, very, very earnestly: This is not a home for my brother man—God's child, one for whom Christ has died. I see in many, perhaps most cases, but one single room where, without a shadow of delicacy, old and young, males and females, sleep promiscuously. Some one with a smile, says: "Talk of the delicacy of slaves!"

Alas! alas! there is none. There is no maiden modesty, no refined manly virtue; and I can not accept the doctrine, that when thus imbruted by the most relentless and persistent energy, the man is treated kindly, because he is fed and clothed in a way to make him an available laborer. In the cabin of the negro I see no book, no culture of taste, no thought. He is an animal well cared for, that he may do good service.

There are men at the North who will treat their oxen and their horses with fiend-like brutality, regardless of the loss of property. There are, of course, such men at the South, beneath whose cruelty the slaves live in perpetual martyrdom. But, as a general rule, all through the United States, beasts of burden, whether human or mere animals, are treated considerately, not only out of regard to their pecuniary value, but also through the instinctive kindness of most hearts.

Were I to take any tiller of the soil in New-England, to the cabin of the negro, show him the sons and daughters of this bondage, and say to him: "Are you willing to accept this as your home for life, and this as the position of your boys and girls?" with indignation he would spurn the insulting question. Were I to take the day-laborer, the humblest mechanic, the barber, the waiter at a hotel, the response would be equally prompt and energetic. Absolutely no one believes that the bondsman is treated well as a *man*, but only as a *slave*.

As we approached the city, the landscape became every hour more attractive; the planters' houses fringing both sides of the stream, in almost an unbroken village. The soil is inexhaustible in its fertility. Soon the spires of the city and the masts of the shipping came in sight. Even New-York can not present so imposing a show, for the crescent form of the river exhibits the merchant fleet, which, at this season of the year, crowds the levee, to the greatest possible advantage. Such an array of steamboats, gorgeous river palaces, from inland ports a thousand miles distant, no other city in the world can show.

I confess that I have but little hope of the peaceful abolition of Slavery. It is estimated that the cotton crop this year will amount to four millions of bales, which, at fifty dollars a bale, comes to two hundred millions of dollars. The sugar crop is estimated at two hundred and fifty thousand hogsheads, which, at seventy dollars a hogshead, amounts to seventeen millions five hundred thousand dollars. This makes a sum total, raised by the slaves, of two hundred and seventeen millions five hundred thousand dollars. This is probably all clear gain, for enough of other things are raised, and enough domestic service performed, to pay for the exceedingly small expenses of the laborers. This sum, though very small, when compared with the industrial and agricultural products of the North, is an immense amount of money to be divided among the comparatively few slave-holders; only about two hundred thousand in number. If, under these circumstances, even those who profess to be Christians, declare the institution to be divinely appointed, what can we hope for from those who make even no pretensions to be disciples of the Saviour?

While human nature remains as it is, therefore, I have but little hope of the peaceful abolition of Slavery. Two conspicuous and immensely important facts are, however, I think, now established. 1. The North, consisting of fifteen or sixteen millions of freemen, to but about six millions in the South, will not consent, under any circumstances whatever, to the extension of this system. That battle has been fought and the victory won. The question is settled forever. The South can now never compete with the North in emigration to new territory. 2. The border States, Missouri, Kentucky, Virginia and Maryland, will soon be drained of their slave population, and must inevitably become Free States. This process is now progressing with a rapidity which is accelerated every month. The whole slave population will soon be crowded into the extreme South. Those who do not like Slavery, will remove to the Free States. What God will then do, no prophet has revealed. May He guide to such councils as shall arrest impending woe.

Sunday Dec. 11.—This is the great market day in the French quarter in New-Orleans. As I was anxious to witness the novel scene, which brings in a large number of plantation negroes with their little ventures for sale, I went down at an early hour of the morning, to the market. The whole scene is most decidedly French, and reminds one of Paris. Still I saw very many less of the plantation negroes than I had expected to see, and very many less than I should have seen a few years ago. Nothing has surprised me more in New-Orleans than the small number of the colored population. When the De Soto was made fast to the levee, the wide and extended plateau was thronged with laborers, but they were nearly all Germans or Irish. Rarely could I see a dark skin. It was the same in the streets as we drove through them. Upon speaking of this to a very intelligent gentleman, he observed that the slaves were becoming so exceedingly profitable upon the plantations, that large numbers had been sold from the city for that purpose; and that also it was found not well to have them associated with free laborers, as they acquired bad notions and restless habits.

Clearly it must be so. The cities, especially the commercial ones, will soon be drained, and the powerful tendency now must be to gather the slaves upon the remote plantations, where they can be excluded from popular view, and no longer be agitated by the sights and the sounds of freedom. There are many secluded plantations now, where there are from five hundred to a thousand slaves. They are never permitted to leave the plantation — never. And no one is permitted to visit them from another plantation—not one. Thus they are buried from the world, and toil in darkness from the cradle to the grave. If their master chance to have a respect for religion, they receive some faint religious instruction. If, as is more probably the case, he is a mere man of the world, they are left to utter heathenism.

In Africa some missionary might reach them. On the plantation of an infidel master there is no hope.

I am struck with the kindness with which the white population address the negroes, and the manifestly friendly relations which generally exist between the two classes. The negrophobia at the North is unknown at the South. This afternoon I went to an African church. A slave preached—a man entirely without culture, but of very vigorous mind. He clearly understood, and touchingly unfolded the plan of salvation through faith in Jesus Christ. I have never been more deeply impressed with the beautiful adaptation of Christianity to the wants of the world. Clay, Webster, Jackson, our strongest, wisest, firmest men, have given the most emphatic utterance to their soul's need of an atoning Saviour. And here rises a poor slave, unlettered, and in the darkest ignorance, so far as human knowledge is concerned, and yet rich in this Christian faith; and as he unfolds a Saviour's love, he sways the hearts of his auditors as no other conceivable theme could move them. My eyes were dim with tears, as in broken language, he spoke of patience under life's cares, and depicted the glory of that world where there shall be no night, and where all tears shall be wiped from every eye. The singing was an extempore wail, without articulate words, such as I never heard before from earthly voices.

A Southern Christian gentleman, who accompanied me, and who sympathized with me in every utterance of the preacher, said, as we came out: "Many of these poor creatures will hereafter be in Abraham's bosom, when, perhaps, some of their present owners may be with Dives imploring a drop of water to cool their tongues."

These slaves, aided undoubtedly by kind Christian friends, for there is much, very much, of true Christian sympathy with them here in the South, have succeeded in building a church which can not have cost less than ten thousand dollars. It was really touching, at the close of the service, to see so many of these young men, born in bondage and in bondage to die, go up through the aisle and lay their contribution of a dime upon the table. I noticed, very accidentally, that the contribution of my Southern friend was five dollars.

Monday morning, Dec. 12. — This day has been like one of the most delightful we experience in May. With an invigorating breeze and bright, warm sunshine, the trees and the shrubbery in full leaf, and the golden oranges and limes blending with the verdure of the gardens, the city looks beautifully. We took a ride, up the river, this morning to Carrolton, about eight miles. The whole distance is almost one continuous village of neat, homelike houses, surrounded with gardens. Many were very attractive. There is diffused all around the most gratifying indications of prosperity and thrift. The city itself is essentially a free city, and all its energy is the energy of freedom.

I met a Northern gentleman this morning, and almost his first words were: "As to this peculiar institution, I was always in favor of slavery when in the North, and I am still more so now that I have come South. The slaves are much better off than the laboring classes at the North." Noticing, perhaps, a look of surprise on my countenance, he added: "The *poor* laboring classes I mean, the *poor* ones."

I can only say that no extent of charity can lead me to believe that there is any sincerity in such a declaration. Our noblest statesmen, our most distinguished clergy, our most accomplished ladies, have often come from the homes of the laboring class at the North. The condition of the slave, under a humane master, is undoubtedly preferable to that of the prostitutes, vagabonds, and thieves at the Five Points in New-York. If this be the eulogy slavery demands, let it not be withheld. But to compare the homes of the farmers, mechanics or day-laborers, in any village of New-England with the cabins of the negroes, is simply absurd.

I observe in this morning's paper the following advertisement, which penetrates the cabin of the negro. How would such an advertisement read in the North, sweeping with its desolation through the homes of those with us, who by the labor of their hands earn their daily bread, tearing away from those homes, for ruthless sale into slavery, fathers and mothers, sisters and brothers:

"AUCTION.

"Tuesday, December 20th, at 12 o'clock, at public auction, at the City Hotel, without reserve, will be sold one hundred and three choice plantation hands; seventy-three likely young men and boys; thirty-five women and girls, single and in families, comprising field hands, mechanics, and house-servants, all classing strictly No. 1. The gang will be at the office of the auctioneers, the day previous to the sale, for the full inspection of the public."

Mechanics, of the North, what say you! Is your condition like this? I see by the same paper that a law has just passed the Legislature of Mississippi, declaring that all the free colored people therein, who do not leave the State by the first of next July, shall be sold into perpetual slavery. I turn to the census and find that there are about a thousand free colored persons in Mississippi. Many of these people, of remote African descent, are as white as any persons in the State; not a few are the sons and daughters of opulent and intelligent planters. And how are these poor people, guilty of no crime, to escape their awful doom; the most awful that can befall a mortal—slavery for themselves and their offspring forever? Here is a little family, perhaps a Christian family, consisting of father, mother, a son, and a daughter; they are poor and friendless and uninstructed. They must traverse on foot, for they have no means to pay their fare in boat or car, a distance of nearly a thousand miles to reach a Free State. They must run the gauntlet of the Slave States, Alabama, Georgia, the Carolinas, and Virginia, where they are liable at every step to be arrested as fugitive slaves. When they arrive in Virginia they are certain to be thus arrested, for the laws imperiously require their arrest as vagabonds, if not slaves. They are thrown into a jail and advertised as runaways. After a few months, no one appearing to claim them, they are sold at auction, to the highest bidder, *to pay their jail expenses!* The father is sent to Texas, the mother to Louisiana, the son to Mississippi, and the daughter to Alabama. They can not write; lost to each other forever, they never hear tidings of each other's fate.

Now Mississippi has passed such a law with a population of free colored people of nearly a thousand. Arkansas has passed a similar law with a free colored population of about six hundred. And the same law has just passed, by an overwhelming majority, the Senate of Missouri, where there is a free colored population of over twenty-six hundred. Thus in the nineteenth century, and in Christian, republican America, more than four thousand free people, guilty of no crime, and accused of no crime, must in dismay, and through sufferings inconceivable, force their way to a cold, distant land, where they have no friends, no employment, and know not what to do — or they, and their children, must be sold into perpetual slavery. Was there ever any thing in the history of nations more awful? Did tyranny ever commit a more atrocious crime? Is this not a dreadful story to be related through the nations of the world, respecting republican America? There are thousands, and hundreds of thousands at the North, who feel degraded by such acts perpetrated in our country; for in the eye of the world we are one people; as much so as are the English or the French. And yet you tell us, brethren of the South, that we have no right to express or to feel any sympathy for these unhappy victims of oppression so dreadful. You will condemn me severely for this expression of my sympathy; and call me, perhaps, an incendiary and fanatic; an inhuman enemy of the South, who deserves to be hung on the branch of the first tree that can be reached. Brethren, believe me, neither burning nor hanging can stifle this sympathy for the oppressed. We can no more help feeling and shuddering and weeping, when we read such tales, than the slave can help recoiling when the brand of red-hot iron burns and smokes upon his flesh.

And what is the excuse for this outrage so unparalleled in the legislation of Christendom? It is simply that this enslaving of the free is necessary, to enable you to hold firmly four millions more of your fellow-men, whom you have already enslaved. Well did Jefferson, the father of American democracy say, and his words are worthy of being pondered:

"Can the liberties of a nation be thought secure, when we have removed their only firm basis: a conviction in the minds of the people that these liberties are the gift of God? that they are not to be violated but by his wrath? Indeed I tremble for my country, when I reflect that God is just; that his justice can not sleep forever; that considering numbers, nature and natural means only, a revolution of the wheel of fortune, an exchange of situations is among possible events; that it may become *probable*, by supernatural interference. The Almighty has no attribute which can take sides with us in such a contest."

Again he says in view of this most execrable system of despotism the world has ever known, and to which democratic America clings with deathless tenacity:

"What an incomprehensible machine is man! who can endure toil, famine, stripes, imprisonment, and death itself, in vindication of his own liberty; and the next moment be deaf to all those motives whose power supported him through his trial, and inflict on his fellow-man a bondage, one hour of which is fraught with more misery than ages of that which he rose in rebellion to oppose."

It is difficult for me to account for such a state of public opinion as will tolerate legislation so utterly infamous. Tell the story in

England and every heart in the island will shudder with horror; and thousands will be incredulous, and say it can not possibly be true. Tell it in France, in Prussia, in Germany, in Italy, and every where it will awaken a cry of surprise, of grief, of execration. There will be but one thought, and that will be that those States which can pass such enactments not only are lapsing, but have already lapsed into utter barbarism.

And yet, strangely, I do not meet this spirit any where in the homes I visit. Who are these legislators? Where do they come from? Who are their constituents? I meet with no one here in the South, who does not regard such legislation essentially as I regard it—who will not say that it is inhuman and unpardonable. Never have I met more fervent and earnest piety than I am continually meeting at the South.

I should like to live with this people as I meet them. They seem kind, generous, warmhearted. I constantly see indications of genuine sympathy with the colored race, such as I rarely see at the North. I find Christians here, and those not few in number, as devoted and as self-denying as any who can be found on earth. And yet such a law as that which has recently passed the Legislature of Mississippi, and by an overwhelming majority, and which has been enacted by a similar majority in Arkansas, and which has also passed the Senate of Missouri, is simply *infernal.*

Perhaps one explanation is found in the fact that I frequently hear Christians say here: "I am disgusted with politics, and for years have had nothing to do with them." Is it possible that the worst part of the slaveholders, with bowie-knives and revolvers, have over-awed the conscientious portion of the community and taken the affairs of state into their own hands? That they edit the papers, attend the conventions, fill the legislative halls, and send their own men to Congress? If it be so, our Southern brethren have made a terrible mistake, and should break these fetters with which they have allowed themselves to be bound. The hopes of republican liberty throughout the world depend upon the success of this Republic. If we fail, farewell to popular freedom. The Christian can have no more imperious duty than his political duties—he can make no mistake more disastrous to the hopes of the world, than to surrender the administration of this government to Satan's employés.

CHAPTER V.

DEVELOPMENTS: SOCIAL, PHILOSOPHICAL, AND POLITICAL.

Tuesday, Dec. 13. — After an exceedingly pleasant visit in New-Orleans, a visit so pleasant that, with great reluctance, I brought it to so speedy a close, I took the cars this afternoon at two o'clock, for Lake Pontchartrain, eight miles distant from the city. The road passes over a country as level as a floor, with the gloomy swamp of pools and bogs on both sides, rank with funereal cypresses. At four o'clock, a very beautiful and well-managed steamer, the Florida, left the pier, which extended far out into the shallow waters of the lake, to run along the shores of this quiet inland sea, and along Mississippi sound, a hundred and sixty miles, to Mobile.

It is now ten o'clock at night, as with my tablet on my knee, I pencil these lines. The night is warm, almost sultry. There is not a ripple upon the water, which reflects with marvelous distinctness every star in the sky; and there is not the slightest movement of that ground-swell which is ever experienced on the ocean. The cabin, a remarkably cheerful and pleasant-looking room, is filled with groups of gentlemen and ladies; some reading, some conversing. They are all entire strangers to me. I have left my *companion of voyage* in New-Orleans, and am returning entirely alone to the North.

The scene from the deck is solitary and somber. We are just now passing through a narrow strait which connects Lake Pontchartrain with Lake Borgne. The outline of the shore, almost on a level with the water, is dimly discernible, with scattered lights, perhaps from the solitary dwellings of the planters, gleaming here and there in the distance; and the horizon in many places is illumined with dull, lurid fires burning in the swamp.

A gang of plantation slaves, men, women and children, probably a recent purchase, were brought on board the boat just before we started, to be taken to some plantation in Alabama. They were coarsely but comfortably clad, and are now asleep by themselves upon a pile of freight, occupying the place usually taken by poor emigrants in Northern ships. In all respects, as to comfort, intelligence, and respectability, they appear about on a level with the poorest class of Irish emigrants.

Several Southern gentlemen, at my side, have been conversing upon John Brown and Harper's Ferry. They have, however, spoken with great sobriety, and without any violence. Still they seem to be sincerely and totally unconscious that there can be any more wrong in enslaving a "nigger," than in harnessing a horse. I observe that every body here, gentlemen, ladies, Christians, speak of the "niggers." To one whose education has been of the Northern type, the Southern state of mind upon this point is absolutely inconceivable. It does not seem to me that they ever really think of them as men and women. And yet they often love them—as much as I love my noble Newfoundland dog, Lion; and that is saying a *great deal*. A man's attachment for a faithful dog is very, very strong. I do not mean by this that they regard the slaves as dogs; but that the kindness they feel for the "niggers" is a peculiar kindness.

Wednesday night, Dec. 14.—As I awoke this morning at six o'clock, our steamer was just entering the Bay of Mobile. In consequence of the shoal water, only vessels of light draft can ascend to the head of the Bay where Mobile is located; and there were at least a hundred large ships, many of them of the first class, loading and unloading by lighters, nearly thirty miles below the city. It was perfectly calm; the sun was rising in a cloudless sky, and the scene presented was one of unusual activity and beauty. There were many steamers traversing the Bay, and the songs of the sailors, loading and unloading the ships, added to the life of the spectacle. During the morning I listened with interest to the conversation of the various groups scattered over our steamer, taking a part, when proper, in the conversation. One of these was sufficiently suggestive to be worthy of record.

During the night, at one of the little, obscure landing-places on the lake, a young planter, about twenty-five years of age, came on board, apparently from a plantation not far back from the shore. He soon rendered himself revoltingly conspicuous by his profaneness and rowdyism. Boon companions speedily gathered around him, and, for some hours, night was rendered hideous by their revelry. In the morning I found him on deck, still in the flush of his debauch. In loud tones, and with a swaggering air, he said:

"When I am dry, I drink whisky; when I am hungry, I drink whisky; when I am hot, I drink whisky; when I am cold, I drink whisky. I just keep pouring it down all the while. I had rather drink whisky than eat or sleep!

"I am going to Mobile for a *bust*. I never expect to get nearer to heaven than I am when I get to Mobile. *If* I don't *bust* it there this afternoon and to-night!

"The damned niggers, if they don't work well while I am gone, they'll get it. I tell you what I do, when I've been gone on a spree. When I go home, if I find the damned niggers have not done a good week's work, I just take 'em and lick 'em like hell—yes, I lick 'em like hell! God Almighty never yet made a nigger that could come it over me!"

These utterances were interlarded with the most horrible oaths imaginable. From various remarks I inferred, that this young man had recently come into the possession of his estate, somewhere in the vicinity, by the death of his father, and that his mother was still living. He has perhaps a hundred slaves, of all varieties of color, men and women, boys and girls, under his sway, in a remote plantation which no eye of civilization ever sees, and where the cry of his victims can reach no Christian ear. After spending a week in Mobile, losing all his money in gambling, his nerves irritated by debauchery, and his spirit maddened by disappointment, he returns to his helpless slaves to wreak his wrath upon them, and to goad them to severer toil to replenish his purse. Their doom is one which it is awful to contemplate.

Now this case is doubtless an exception. There were perhaps twenty other planters on board, and I did not see another one, who did not seem to me to be a mild and humane man. Still there must be not a few of such exceptions. Good men at the South abhor this, as do good men at the North. But these outrages can only be abolished by abolishing the system which legalizes them. And when we urge our Southern brethren to abandon this system, fraught with such woes, *men at the North*, men of culture and opulence, will lift up their voices and say: "This system of slavery need not be abolished. It is alike advantageous to the slave and his master. *It is just, wise, and beneficent.*"

Brethren of the South, we do by no means feel that you are sinners beyond all others. You can not have worse men with you, than we have with us. There are many at the North, eager at any moment to engage in the slave-trade; many who, if they could get plantations, would treat their slaves more severely than any of you do. And, for this reason, we feel that we have much to do at the North in casting light upon this subject.

We read of the beauties of the Patriarchal Institution, but I think all must admit that this young planter, to whom I have referred, is rather a curious specimen of one of the descendants of the Patriarch. I apprehend, that the Father of the Faithful would feel some reluctance in surrendering his Household to so degenerate a child.

I am a democrat, in every fibre of my soul a democrat, using that much-abused word in its true, classical, sacred sense. My democracy is the democracy which our Saviour Jesus Christ has taught us. He has given me the motto which I inscribe upon my banner: "As ye would that others should do unto you, do ye unto them also."

This is a democracy which embraces *all* in its regards, the whole human family, saint and sinner, rich and poor, bond and free; which would guide and bless Agrippa and Pilate, and the opulent Joseph of Arimathea, and also the poor Magdalen, and the widow who had but two mites. But it is a democracy which has a *peculiar sympathy* for the poor, the friendless, the oppressed; which would restore to every one, however defrauded, his rights; which would stop at the gate to dress the wounds of Lazarus, instead of rushing eagerly in at the palace-door to feast with Dives; which would feed the hungry and clothe the naked, rather than bow in adulation before him who is clothed in purple and fine linen and fares sumptuously every day. It is a democracy devoted rather to the service of the toiling millions than to courting the smiles of the millionaire; which would rather carry comfort to the cabin of the slave than share in the luxuries of the saloon of his master. This is true, heaven-born democracy. There is none other. Every thing else assuming the name is pretense and a sham.

I saw in a paper, which I read in New-Orleans, that a Southern member of Congress stated on the floor of the House, that Thomas Jefferson, in the Declaration of Independence, had no idea of including the colored race in the statement, that,

"All men are endowed by their Creator with certain inalienable rights; that among these are life, liberty, and the pursuit of happiness."

This Southern gentleman declares, that, in this statement, Jefferson intended to include only the white or Caucasian race, and had not the slightest intention of bringing the colored races within the sweep of this principle. And, very defiantly, he challenges any man to rise and say, that Jefferson intended to include the colored races in his Declaration of the Rights of Man.

Now, most peremptorily, do I join issue with you, my friend, upon this point. I aver, that

Jefferson understood, wonderfully well, the use of language; and when he wrote, "*all men*," he meant *all men*, the human family. He thought not of Blumenbach's division of this family into Caucassians, Indians, Ethiopians, Mongolians, and Malays; or of the fifty other classes into which other physiologists have endeavored to classify our race. He did not intend to exclude John Randolph from this principle, because the blood of the Indian circulated in his veins, or Rammohun Roy, because of his Mongolian descent, or Alexander Dumas, because his high genius is inspired by the commingling of Ethiopian and Caucasian blood. It was the *human family* which was in his mind's eye when he gave to the world this noble utterance; and it is an insult to his memory to suggest, that, when drawing up that magnificent bill of rights, the gospel of democracy, which no infidel cavils can ever undermine, his mind was groping about among the trivialities of artificial classifications of our race into white men, and red men, and black men, and yellow men, and tawny men. Jefferson said, "*all*," *all men*. He meant what he said.

The gentleman making this strange affirmation in Congress, necessarily proposes that the Declaration of Independence should be amended to read thus.

"All men of Caucasian blood, that is, men of white complexion, straight hair, small heel-bones and blunt shins, are endowed by their Creator with certain inalienable rights; among these are life, liberty, and the pursuit of happiness."

Does any man, in his senses, believe that Thomas Jefferson would accept this amendment?

I contend that this point is so clear, that there is no room for serious debate. All that Jefferson has written is in accordance with this view. With no prospective fear of the Dred Scott decision, a decision which, in my judgment, will constitute one of the blackest pages in the records of the nineteenth century, he calls the colored people his fellow-*citizens*, recognizing no difference between them and others.

"The whole commerce between master and slave," he indignantly writes, "is a perpetual exercise of the most boisterous passions—the most unremitting despotism on the one part, and degrading submissions on the other.' . . . .

"And with what execration should the statesman be loaded, who, permitting *one half of the citizens thus to trample on the rights of the other*, transforms *those* into despots, and *these* into enemies; destroys the morals of one part, and the *amor patriæ* (love of country) of the other; for, if a slave can have a country in this world, it must be any other in preference to that in which he is born to live and labor for another; in which he must lock up the faculties of his nature, contribute, as far as depends on his individual exertions, to the evanishment of the human race, or entail his own miserable condition on the endless generations proceeding from him."*

* *Notes on Virginia*, p. 40.

Thus pathetically and indignantly does he deplore the doom of one half of his *fellow-citizens*, the slaves, trampled upon by the other half, their masters.

But the sympathy of Jefferson, our great Democratic leader, does not stop here. He calls these oppressed children of bondage not only his fellow-citizens, but his *brethren*.

"We must wait," says he devoutly, "with patience, the workings of an overruling Providence, and hope that that is preparing the deliverance of *these, our brethren!* When the measure of their tears shall be full, when their groans shall have involved heaven itself in darkness, doubtless a God of justice will awaken to their distress. Nothing is more certainly written in the Book of Fate, than that this people shall be free."

And these were not hasty views, or views which he subsequently abandoned. But six weeks before his death, in a letter addressed to James Heaton, he writes:

"My sentiments have been *forty years* before

the public. Had I repeated them forty times, they would only become the more stale and thread-bare. Although I shall not live to see them consummated, they will not die with me."

It is in vain to aver that Jefferson wished for freedom, only for the *Caucasian race*. It is in vain to deny that Jefferson is the chief leader of those whom you, brethren of the South, now call incendiaries and fanatics. It is in vain to deny that his Declaration of Independence, his Letters, his Notes on Virginia, are papers which you now pronounce to be incendiary documents, and which you forbid white non-slaveholders at the South to read, or the mails to carry. And lastly, and most sadly, it is in vain to deny that were Jefferson now to utter these sentiments in Eastern Virginia, the Carolinas, or Georgia, he would expose himself to all the insult and outrage of lynch-law.

A poor Irish stone cutter, James Power, at work on the State House in Columbia, South-Carolina, recently ventured to remark, that he thought Slavery objectionable, inasmuch as it caused the white laborer at the South to be regarded as an inferior and degraded man.

The alarming statement was reported to the vigilance committee, consisting of twelve persons. The poor Irishman was arrested, led through the main street of the city by an immense crowd, hooting and yelling. Two negroes were compelled to drag him through the puddles and muddy places, to the State House yard. A mob of three thousand was assembled around him. He was stripped to the skin; and a stout negro was ordered, with a cow-hide, to lay thirty-nine lashes on his bare back, which should draw blood at every stroke. After enduring the dreadful anguish of this infliction, he was daubed with tar, hair, eye-brows, body and all, and then was covered with feathers and cotton. His pants were then drawn up over his limbs to the waist, and he was thrust into the negro-car, and sent out of the State.*

As we read such narratives of which the

* The *Charleston Mercury* boasts of this achievement.

Southern papers boast, we are led to inquire, have we indeed become a nation of barbarians? Is our religion, and is our civilization clean gone forever? We search the papers of every nation in Europe in vain, for any thing approaching such savage and shocking inhumanity. European gentleman read such recitals, and are lost in utter amazement; and they know not where to look for the influences which have thus converted civilized men into ferocious and brutal monsters.

What is the crime of which we are guilty, who deplore with Jefferson, the existence of Slavery, and plead and pray for its peaceful abolition? Brethren of the South! we have learned our lesson from the wisest, the purest, the most patriotic of your own number. Was Jefferson a Fanatic, an Incendiary, and an Enemy of the South? We can not feel more deeply than he felt, or speak more earnestly.

The New-York *Independent* of Dec. 29, 1859, gives a narrative of the event, taken from the lips of the sufferer, whose wounds were still unhealed.

Was Patrick Henry a Fanatic, an Incendiary, an Enemy of the South? And yet he addresses to you, and bequeaths to us these burning words:

"Times that seem to have pretensions to boast of high improvements in the arts and sciences, and refined morality, have brought into general use, and guarded by many laws a species of violence and tyranny, which our more rude and barbarous, but more honest ancestors detested. Is it not amazing that at a time when the rights of humanity are defined, and understood with precision, in a country above all others fond of liberty, that, in such an age and such a country, we find men, professing a religion the most mild, humane, gentle and generous, adopting such a principle as repugnant to humanity as it is inconsistent with the Bible, and destructive to liberty? Every thinking, honest man, rejects it in speculation."

Was John Randolph of Roanoke, a Fanatic, and an Incendiary, and an Enemy of the

South? And yet, in the solemn hour, when death and judgment were opening to his view, he writes in his last will and testament.

"I give to my slaves their freedom, to which my conscience tells me they are justly entitled. It has a long time been a matter of the deepest regret to me, that the circumstances under which I inherited them, and the obstacles thrown in the way by the laws of the land, have prevented my emancipating them in my life-time; which it is my full intention to do in case I can accomplish it."

I seem to see this extraordinary man rise from the grave, and with his long, bony finger, point to an orator on the boards of the Music Hall, at the great Union Saving meeting, in New-York. With his peculiar sneer, he repeats the words pronounced in eulogy of Slavery. "It is just, wise and beneficent." And then vibrating that finger, and curling his lip with scorn, he repeats his well-known words, uttered on the floor of Congress:

"Sir, I envy neither the heart nor the head

of that man from the North, who rises to defend Slavery on principle."

Was Henry Clay a Fanatic, and an Incendiary, and an Enemy of the South, when he exclaimed in tones which still vibrate upon the nation's ear:

"So long as God allows the vital current to flow through my veins, I will never, *never*, NEVER, by word or thought, by mind or will, aid in admitting one rood of free territory to the *everlasting curse* of human bondage!"*

Was Governor McDowell of Virginia, a Fanatic, and an Incendiary, and an Enemy of the South, when, in the Legislature of Virginia, he gave utterance to the pathetic and forceful words:

"Who that looks to this unhappy bondage of an unhappy people, in the midst of our society, and thinks of its incidents or issues, but weeps over it as a curse as great upon him who inflicts it, as upon him who suffers it?

---

* Speech in the United States Senate in 1850.

Sir, you may place the slave where you please —you may dry up, to the uttermost, the fountains of his feelings, the springs of his thought, you may close upon his mind every avenue of knowledge, and cloud it over with artificial night—you may yoke him to your labors as the ox that liveth only to work, and worketh only to live—you may put him under any process which, without destroying his value as a slave, will debase and crush him as a rational being—you may do this, and the idea that he was born to be free will survive it all. It is allied to his hope of immortality; it is the ethereal part of his nature which oppression can not rend. It is a torch lit up in his soul by the hand of Deity, and never meant to be extinguished by the hand of man."

Was the illustrious Virginian, Thomas Marshall, of Fauquier, a Fanatic, an Incendiary, and an Enemy of the South, when he, in the same Legislature of Virginia, of 1832, replied to the question, "Wherefore then object to Slavery?" in the ponderous words:

"Because it is ruinous to the whites—retards improvements, roots out an industrious population, banishes the yeomanry of the country, deprives the spinner, the weaver, the smith, the shoemaker, the carpenter, of employment and support."

And, finally, was George Washington a Fanatic, and an Incendiary, and an enemy to the South, when he wrote to Robert Morris, April 12, 1786:

"I can only say that there is not a man living, who wishes more sincerely than I do to see a plan adopted for the abolition of it," (Slavery.)

Or when he wrote to Lafayette, April 5, 1788:

"The scheme, my dear Marquis, which you propose as a precedent, to encourage the emancipation of the black people in this country, from the state of bondage in which they are held, is a striking evidence of the benevolence of your heart. I shall be happy to join you in so laudable a work."

In his last will and testament he inscribed these noble words:

"Upon the decease of my wife, it is my will and desire that all the slaves which I hold in my own right, shall receive their freedom. To emancipate them during her life would, though earnestly wished by me, be attended with such insuperable difficulties, on account of their mixture by marriage with the dower negroes, as to excite the most painful sensation, if not disagreeable consequences, from the latter, while both descriptions are in the occupancy of the same proprietor, it not being in my power, under the tenure by which the dower negroes are held, to manumit them."

Mrs. Washington, immediately after her husbands death, learning from his will that the only obstacle to the immediate emancipation of the slaves was her right of dower, immediately relinquished that right, and the slaves were at once emancipated.

Brethren of the South, we are not Fanatics, and Incendiaries, and your Enemies, because we have imbibed the spirit of these noble Southerners. It is from their lips that we have learned our lessons of liberty. Their teachings have instructed us to abhor Slavery. I close this chapter with the solemn words of the Father of our Country.

"I never mean, unless some particular circumstances should compel me to it, to possess another slave by purchase; it being among my *first wishes* to see some plan adopted by which Slavery, in this country may be abolished by law."

"*Abolished!*" Washington was an abolitionist! and there are thousands, and tens of thousands at the North, who have been instructed in his school. The lessons he has taught them they will never forget.

CHAPTER VI.

THE RIVER, THE PEOPLE, THE HOMES.

Thursday, Dec. 15.—At eleven o'clock yesterday I reached Mobile. Hospitable friends there took me to their house to dine, and in the afternoon I rode through the city and its suburbs. The day was unusually fine, and to me the city looked exceedingly attractive. Here, as in New-Orleans, I was surprised to see how effectually free labor seems to have driven slave labor from the wharves and the streets. The city, with its intelligence and its enterprise, is a dangerous place for the slave. He acquires knowledge of human rights, by working with others who receive wages when he receives none; who can come and go at their pleasure, when he, from the cradle to the grave, must obey a master's imperious will. It is found ex-

THE RIVER—PEOPLE—HOMES. 113

pedient, almost necessary, to remove the slave from these influences, and send him back to the intellectual stagnation and gloom of the plantation.

The Irish and the Germans seem to do nearly all the work of the streets. White girls are being also more and more employed in domestic service; and I think that but a few years will pass away ere nearly all of the colored population will be removed from the *cities* of the South. Indeed, now, New-Orleans and Mobile seem but little more like slave cities than do Philadelphia and New-York.

Mobile and its environs are almost perfectly flat, but it has the peculiar beauty of the prairie. There were a great many homes which looked attractive, and as though any one might love to live there; and from the appearance of these homes, with front yards and shrubbery and flowers, I am sure that the society here, must be pleasant. The country, in the extreme South, is far more attractive to me than I had expected to find it. The yellow-fever epidemic is a very serious drawback to the idea of a residence in Mobile. Were it not for this, it seems to me that beneath its sunny skies, any man might love to find his home.

The society I meet here is frank and agreeable. Indeed it seems to me that there must be two classes of Southerners, as different from each other as light is from darkness. I often wonder if our brethren at the South are bewildered by the same apparent diversity of character in our Northern men. The Southerners whom I meet at the South in social intercourse, to whom I am introduced at hotels, in steamboats, and at the fire-side, are genial, friendly, courteous—gentlemen in tone, kind and polished in manners, ever recognizing the courtesies of refined society. But there is another class whom I never meet, whom I seek for in vain, but who are revealed to me in newspaper editorials, in convention speeches, and in Congressional debates. The difference between these two classes is so vast as to excite astonishment. From what I read I should infer that there was a very numerous class at the South, composing the great majority of its population, whose mothers had fed them in infancy, if I may quote an expression of Festus, on "buttered thunder."

I am led to these remarks by a few paragraphs I have observed in one of the newspapers. It is reported that one of the Governors of one of the Southern States has said in Convention:

"As for me, I mean to stay here, with one exception. If invasion shall ever again cross the Northern border of Virginia, and I can get one hundred men, ay, or ten men, to follow me, whether the Legislature authorizes it or not, I will go North; and, if the Southern people are the men of will I take them to be, rather than let this Union be dissolved they will drive into Canada every Black Republican, every abolitionist, every disunionist."

Now, happy as we shall be to receive such allies in defense of the Union we love, and which we desire so earnestly to have preserved, there is something really appalling in such a menace. Ferocity like this seems to our cold Northern blood absolutely awful. It is said that when the African lion roars, his terrific voice swells over hill and valley, filling a circle six miles in diameter, and that every living thing within the circle, whether man or beast, trembles at the sound.

But there is something more fearful, even than this, in the very idea of this invasion of the North by ten men—taking Philadelphia by storm; then by sudden resistless assault demolishing Cincinnati, New-York, Boston, and Buffalo; and then driving some ten or fifteen millions of people from their cities, their villages, their peaceful homes, hundreds of miles to the wastes of Canada, and then precipatating them pell-mell into the St. Lawrence. It is awful! It is heart-rending! There is that in the very thought of this which makes one's lips turn pale, causes the hair of the head to stand on end, and freezes the blood in one's veins with horror. What awful ferocity these ten men must possess! What demoniac fierceness and energy and power! Milton's description of the fierce fight of the fallen angels, pales into insignificance before their achievements.

It is difficult to account for the fact that one never meets any of these fierce creatures in his travels. I have not met with a single one. I have seen, of course, some uncultivated men, some poor and debased, some profane men, but I have met with not a single specimen of this kind of character; and I can truly say that almost every Southerner whom I have thus far seen, has seemed to me a courteous, unassuming, kind-hearted gentlemen. I expected to have caught a glimpse of some of these creatures, tearing over the hills like a locomotive under an attack of delirium-tremens. But thus far I have been disappointed. I have met with many, who were truly genial companions, and whom any gentleman would love as intimate associates and neighbors and friends. Do those fierce men, who utter such terrible menaces, like lions, sleep in their lair by day, and never come out but in the night?

It is now late at night. I am writing in the cabin of the steamer. The boat is crowded, apparently with Southern planters; but I have not yet heard a word or witnessed an action inconsistent with the usages of reputable society. We are still breasting the current of the Alabama river, having ascended nearly two hundred miles since yesterday afternoon. The scenery soon becomes a little monotonous, though the general aspect of the country is rich and very beautiful. The climate must be delightful, and, were the institutions of man what they should be, the whole region might be as a garden of loveliness. But since we left Mobile I have seen only two houses which would be deemed inhabitable by a respectable white family at the North. We may have passed hundreds in the night, but I have not seen them.

I am informed that the fever-and-ague prevails upon the banks of the river, so that the beautiful sites on the bluffs are neglected, and the planters build back, in what are called the "piney woods," where they find pure air and good water. The plantations, however, extend along the rich bottom-lands of the river, where the soil is inexhaustibly fertile; and the negroes' cabins are erected near the shore, where they can have access to abundance of water, such as it is, and can be near their work. Their huts, to me, look wretched in the extreme, with not a pane of glass, not a particle of green turf, not a flower or a shrub, not an out-building of any kind, not the slightest indication of any thing which we, at the North, call comfort. What do people mean by saying that the negroes at the South are better provided for than the laboring population at the North?

Miserable, indeed, must the life be, the mere animal life, spent in these dirty, cheerless cabins. There are no resources of any kind for mental culture, no books, no furniture; no pure mother's loving guidance, no intelligent father's instructions. They are merely cabins where "niggers" can be fed and sheltered, so as to be kept in good working order.

We passed this afternoon one large and beautiful mansion, which would be deemed beautiful any where. It occupied a very commanding position, and with its cupola, verandah, white fence, green blinds, and shrubbery, reminded one of those pleasant homes which are seen in countless thousands in the Northern States. It was such a house as with us would cost perhaps ten thousand dollars. The owner was evidently a man of thrift. His plantation was large, piles of cotton-bales were collected on the shore, waiting for a steamer to take them to Mobile. Groups of negroes, of all ages, and both sexes, coarse, soulless-looking creatures, were scattered around, watching the passage of the boat. This is the only house I *have seen* since leaving Mobile, for a distance of more than two hundred miles, in which I think I could be willing to live.

And yet, this must be rather a gloomy home. There is no church here, no village school, no singing-meeting, no social winter-evening gatherings. The soil is so soft and rich, that for much of the year the roads are quite impassable. The proprietor may find enough to occupy him in the care of his vast estate. But to the sons and daughters, the home must be almost like a cloister. But the whole region is beautiful, very, very beautiful. It is still eminently a new country, with probably not one tenth of the land as yet under cultivation. When thriving towns shall fringe these shores, now mainly covered with forest, and pleasant villages; and farm-houses, with churches and schools, and all the appliances of high enlightenment shall embellish the interior, this country will be like a garden, unsurpassed, perhaps, by any other on the globe. But it is clear that this can only be accomplished by the energy of free institutions. Where the masses of the people are degraded, ignorant, and, consequently, thriftless, the general aspect of the country *must be* miserable.

The scenes which we witness at night are often exceedingly wild, and weird-like in the extreme. The boat frequently arrives at some obscure landing. The whistle is blown just before our arrival, which brings a group of half-dressed negroes tumbling down the bank to see what is going on. In a sort of iron frame-work basket, with a long handle, chips of pitch-pine knots are placed, which are set in a blaze, and which instantly produce almost the most brilliant torch imaginable. The forests, the dark flowing river, the barbaric-looking negroes, the boatmen, the shouts, and the lurid flames of the torches, all produce a spectacle, which I never weary in beholding.

Friday, Dec. 16.—A dark wet day, and the rain falling in floods. We have spent the whole day ascending the river, which is so tortuous in its course, that, though it is but two hundred miles by land from Mobile to Montgomery, it is four hundred miles by water. And yet the land route is so exceedingly uncomfortable, leading through miry roads, or over corduroy bridges, that nearly all the travel is in the boats. The scenery of the river soon, from its sameness, ceases to interest, since there are no cheerful villages, or church spires, or pleasant-looking homes to gratify the eye. We see nothing but the sweep of the forest, with frequent expanses of cotton fields, now looking dry and dead, and occasional groups of forlorn-looking negro-cabins. To think of a lifetime spent in such a hut, cut off from all mental culture, from all joys, but eating corn bread, and sleeping on straw, is awful.

It is a mystery unfathomable, how a Christian, who believes that God made man but little lower than the angels, and that Christ came to redeem and to elevate him even above the condition from which he has fallen, can regard with any feelings but those of utter abhorrence, a system which thus shuts up millions to ignorance and barbarism.

There are no Bibles in these cabins, no Sabbath-schools, and it must be very rare, indeed, that there can be any preached gospel. The intelligence of these plantation slaves, thus studiously excluded from every gleam of moral and intellectual light, must be almost inconceivably low. The slaves in the cities, working in the midst of the conversation of white men, listen eagerly, and gain some information. This has alarmed their masters, and they are sending them off, as fast as possible, to the plantations where, as in a tomb, no sight or sound of knowledge can reach them. A few years ago, the levee at New-Orleans was covered with slaves, loading and unloading the ships. But the poor creatures were gaining information, and their masters took the alarm. Now, hardly a colored face is to be seen on the levee, and the work there is done by the Germans and the Irish.

"The cities," said a gentleman to me, "is no place for the niggers. They get strange notions into their heads, and grow discontented. They ought, every one of them, to be sent back on to the plantations."

This process is now going on with exceeding rapidity. Even now, a person may take the tour of the United States, and hardly see any thing of Slavery. He will see well-dressed servants in the hotels, and petted maid-servants waiting upon kind mistresses. The miseries of the plantation are remote from his eye. There is great alarm felt in the South in view of the enterprise and energy the negro is developing, and from the light which is penetrating his mind from the abundance which floods our country. His energies must be crushed. The eyes of his mind must be so far blinded, as only to give him sufficient light to enable him to work. No one will deny that such is the fact, though, perhaps, some may deem it unkind to say it.

CHAPTER VII.

ENERGY OF THE BLACKS AND SLAVERY OF THE WHITES.

Saturday night, Dec. 17.—At five o'clock last evening, in a pouring rain, we arrived at Montgomery. The city is said to be very beautiful, but I had no opportunity to view its attractions. It is a small place of but a few thousand inhabitants, very pleasantly located. Notwithstanding the rain, I contrived to visit the Artesian well, which pours forth an unintermitted stream of very clear, luke-warm water, from a depth of several hundred feet. It is supposed by geologists that the interior of the earth, after piercing the crust for forty miles, is a lake of liquid fire. The molten mass is often ejected from volcanoes, the chimneys of this mighty furnace; and the lower we sink our wells, after we get beyond the influence of the sun, the nearer we approach these fires, and the hotter we find the water which rises. In many places springs gush up from such depths that the water is ever boiling with the excessive heat.

After taking a very comfortable supper at the St. Charles Hotel, we took the cars, at nine o'clock, for Augusta, Georgia. The night was exceedingly dark, and the rain descended in floods, which seemed really appalling. There were many fears that some of the culverts might have been washed away, and that we should before morning encounter some serious disaster. But all night long, through the rain and the darkness, we went careering on in perfect safety; and with the dawn of the morning found ourselves approaching the frontiers of Georgia.

The country itself, so far as hills and vales, forests and streams, climate and soil, are concerned, is very beautiful. But man has done but little to add to its attractions. Almost wherever you encounter the work of his hands, in the rural districts, you see a deformity. With a region so richly endowed by nature, with a country so wonderfully adapted to be the home of opulence, intelligence, refinement, and joy, one feels disappointed and pained to meet only forlorn-looking villages, miserable negro huts, and a white population sunk almost below the negro, and seemingly content with a degree of indolence and discomfort which hardly entitles them to the name of civilized beings. Occasionally we passed a dilapidated building, which the genius of ugliness must have exhausted its energies in erecting, and which we were told was a church. It is to be hoped that the worshippers are not to be judged by the aspect of their shrines. The Southern country churches! Did civilization ever before witness such edifices! It is said that a Southern infidel once impiously remarked, that he thought that they were "good enough for the worship of One who was born in a manger."

At Atlanta I procured a morning paper, the *Southern Confederacy*, of Dec. 17. It contains a petition to the Legislature of Georgia, which confirms some of the views I have presented. I quote the following passages:

"We beg leave to represent to your honorable bodies, that the allowing slaves to hire their own time, to live apart from their masters, to own cabs, drays, baggage-waggons, and use them for their own use—to take contracts for work as mechanics, is a great evil. We, your petitioners, earnestly request that a law shall be passed, prohibiting any negroes from living off the premises where their masters reside; prohibiting any negro from taking a contract to erect a building, or do any other mechanical labor; and providing that they shall not work as mechanics or otherwise, except under the immediate direction of their owners, or white men, to whom they may be hired; prohibiting, also, that no negro shall own or drive a cab, dray, wagon, or other public vehicle, or run such public vehicle for himself, and to his profit wholly or in part."

What a comment is this upon the declaration, that the negro is so lazy, that he will not work unless driven by the lash! Here the whole legislative power of the State of Georgia is invoked to paralyze the energies of the negro seeking employment, through the most chilling repulses and discouragements. No language can be too severe to denounce a system which demands such atrocious legislation. We hazard nothing in saying that the pages of history may be searched in vain to find a code more utterly infamous than the slave code of the Southern States. And this in Republican, Christian America, and in the nineteenth century!

It is indeed depressing to contemplate this Southern country in its thriftlessness, desolation, and debasement—and think what it might be were man but true to himself. I can conceive of no agriculture more pleasant, more attractive in every respect, than the culture of cotton. Let this whole region be cut up into farms of between one and two hundred acres; let free labor rear her tasteful dwellings, such as she has reared by hundreds of thousands in Ohio, in Connecticut, in Maine, let each farmer, in addition to raising the supplies his family may need, also raise, say twenty bales of cotton, which would afford even his young children employment and pleasure, and which would bring him in at fifty dollars a bale, one thousand dollars in cash, and what a vision of beauty immediately blooms over these now scathed fields! Farm-houses, orchards, gardens, villages, school-houses, academies, church spires, printing-presses, book-stores, would rise as by magic, and the desert would blossom as the rose. These regions, under such institutions, might be converted into the glory of our country and the world.

There is so much work to be done that we need the labor of every colored man now in the South. None could be spared. The proprietors will need them as hired laborers in their fields. The matrons will need the females as cooks, and washer-women, and dairy-maids; and can afford to pay them wages which will incite their industry, and rouse their ambition. A fallen race can not be raised in a day. These negroes must long be employed in the humble avocations of life. But industry and labor are ever elevating and ennobling. It is Slavery only which debases and crushes the soul. Let us but take this colored population by the hand, awaken within them self-respect, employ them in all service, domestic, agricultural, and mechanical, for which they can show adaptation; encourage them to establish schools for the education of their children, instruct them to rear cheerful cottages, and to embellish them with shrubbery and flowers; lead them to the Sabbath-school and the church, and we shall need no oppressive laws to drive them out of the country as nuisances. The colored man needs, in his depressed condition, the white man—he needs his fostering care, the guidance of his superior intelligence, the protection of his laws.

The white man needs the aid of his colored brother, as his assistant, or his servant in the house, the field, or the shop. Change the relation from slave labor to free, hired labor, and every colored man at the South becomes of increased value to the country. Under these circumstances such a flood of white population would pour in beneath the sunny skies of the South, as soon to destroy the present disproportion between the whites and the blacks, and, ere long, there would be the entire evanishing of the cloud which now menaces our land.

Satan is a hard master. He lures us to oppression, and then curses us in our crime. God shows us the path of rectitude, and it is the path of prosperity and joy.

Let none say that the negroes will not work for wages. The petition to the Georgia Legislature silences that falsehood forever. The slaves are so eager to work for wages that even when they have to hire their time, paying two thirds of their wages to their masters, they will still press on so earnestly, learning mechanic trades, taking contracts, purchasing horses and drays, that the proud, rich, intelligent white race feels called upon to interpose legislative enactments to crush their energies! It is not necessary to utter another word upon this point. The *horrible* petition to the Georgia Legislature must silence the most inveterate caviler.

Let no one say that white men can not labor beneath a Southern sun. Look at those Germans and Irish working with such energy upon the heated levee at New-Orleans. Look at those crowds of white men straining every nerve upon the quay at Mobile, and loading and unloading ships beneath the full blaze of the sun, on the glassy waters of the bay. Will they admit that negroes can beat them in their work? Go with me to Texas! Look at those vast cotton-fields, cultivated entirely by white labor, and will you still say that the white man can not work at the South?

Now just let me crush the head of this slander, till the tail of it even shall never squirm again. It has lived long enough, and done mischief enough. It is time that it should die. For years we have been grossly slandering the beautiful South, the *Italy* of our country—alas! the Italy in more senses than one—by the assertion, that the climate is so unsalubrious that a white man can not labor there.

1. There are already at the South more than one million of free white laborers, engaged in agriculture, working in the fields, exclusive of those engaged in the mechanic arts, and they experience no more difficulty than do workmen at the North. Indeed cases of *coup de soleil*, or being sun-struck, are far more numerous at the North than at the South. In fact the intensity of heat in Maine is greater, the mercury rises higher, than in South-Carolina. The more moderate heat of the South is more prolonged; that is all. Labor in the open sun is never so perilous there as in our hottest August days.

2. By the census it appears that in Alabama there are now sixty-seven thousand white men, who work habitually tilling the soil; that in Mississippi there are fifty-five thousand; and in

Texas, forty-seven thousand, thus industriously at work in the fields. Is not this trying the experiment satisfactorily? Is not the question settled?

3. The climate of the South is the climate of Southern Europe, where no white man ever thinks of complaining that the heat is too great for labor. In fact there can hardly be a more genial climate for the introduction of all sorts of labor than that which our Southern States present.

4. Listen to the voice of testimony: "In the extreme South," says Cassius M. Clay, " at New-Orleans, the laboring men, the stevedores and hackmen on the levee, where the heat is intensified by the proximity of the red brick buildings, are all white men, and they are in the full enjoyment of health.

"But how about cotton? I am informed by a friend of mine, himself a slaveholder, that in north-western Texas. among the German settlements, who, true to their national instincts, will not employ the labor of a slave, they produce more cotton to the acre, and of a better quality, than that produced by slave labor." Is not Texas far enough South to test this question?

"The steady heat of our summers," says Governor Hammond, of South-Carolina, "is not so prostrating as the short, but frequent and sudden, bursts of Northern summers."

"Here, in New-Orleans," says Dr. Cartwright, "the larger part of the drudgery, work requiring exposure to the sun, as railroad-making, street-paving, dray-driving, ditching, and building, is performed by white people."

One of the ex-Governors of Alabama told me that any labor whatever the negro could perform in Alabama, the white man could perform still more efficiently. We might multiply this evidence indefinitely. But it is abundant. We are greatly deceived at the North in reference to the extreme heat of the Southern climate, as our Southern friends are in reference to the unbearable cold at the North. South-Carolina is not burning beneath an equatorial sun, nor Maine freezing in Arctic ices. The mercury in Maine not unfrequently rises to 96°, in the shade; while ice at Galveston, Texas, has formed three inches in thickness, snow five feet in depth has spread over the fields of North-Carolina, ice ten inches thick has covered her streams; and many men have been frozen to death on the prairies of Louisiana, Mississippi, and Texas. The whole expanse of our Southern States is within the circuit of the temperate zone, presenting as attractive a field for human industry as mortals can desire.

Sabbath, Dec. 18. *Augusta, Georgia.*—Weary of travel, I have stopped to pass the Sabbath in this city, and it is indeed, notwithstanding a little of an uncared-for aspect, one of the most beautiful cities in our land. In the morning I attended the first Presbyterian Church. It is a pleasant house, was well filled with a very intelligent-looking audience, and a young man preached a sermon, thoroughly evangelical in its character. No where have I seen indications of a better observed Sabbath. I was much struck with the peculiarly neat dress, and happy aspect of the negro children in the streets. Most of the blacks I met seemed highly intelligent, and very respectable. It does seem a shame that laws should be called for to crush their energies as they strive to rise to manhood. Poor creatures! The atmosphere of the city is too life-giving, and creates thought. It is the doom of them all to be sent back to the gloom of the plantation-cabin. Here the very signs over the shop-doors teach them to read, and they must be sent where no rays of light can penetrate their minds. May God pity them. "There is no flesh in man's obdurate heart."

I am more and more impressed with the grandeur of our country. It is a world by itself. I have now been traveling day and night, since last Tuesday, on one of the great routes between New-Orleans and New-York, and have not yet got half-way home. The distance we have already passed is over nine hundred miles. I leave here in the cars at eight o'clock to-morrow morning, and must travel day and night until Wednesday, to reach Washington. Our country is also as highly favored in fertility of soil, salubrity of climate, variety of products, and beauty of scenery, as it is in grandeur. We need but intelligence and piety to make us the greatest and happiest people on the globe.

It is a great mistake on the part of our Southern brethren, to imagine that the North feels that *its* interests would be promoted by the decay of the South. Portland is not clad in sackcloth, because the bells of prosperity are ringing in Boston. Massachusetts is not abandoned to briers and desolation, because Ohio is blooming like a rose. Hawks and owls do not build their nests upon grass-grown wharves in New-York, because the floods of prosperous life roll along the levee of New-Orleans. The thrift, wealth, and power of our whole country is promoted by the prosperity of each portion of it. Just so far as each individual man rises in the scale of intelligence, and in the gratification of expanded and healthful desires, just in that proportion does he add to the prosperity of the whole country. The South would not be enriched, but fearfully impoverished, were the North suddenly to degenerate into semi-barbarism, and were her cities and her plains reduced to solitude, or roamed over by such a mere animal population as floods Central Asia.

And were the South suddenly to emerge into tenfold wealth; were ships to crowd all her ports, and beautiful villages smile in all her sunny meadows, and fringe all her luxuriant streams with churches, and schools, and free presses, and libraries, and the music of the ringing hammer, and the hum of ten thousand looms, it would not be sectional, but national prosperity and power. The shout of gratulation would be echoed back from the mountains of Maine, to the plantations of Louisiana. A kind Providence has so ordered affairs, that the healthful prosperity of every man tends to promote the prosperity of every other man. Individual towns, counties, states and nations, all help each other by every step that is made in the direction of energy and thrift. The cars of the New-York Central roll more majestically along, because the trains on the Illinois Central are freighted with the wealth of an empire.

No one can pass through our Southern States, and not be saddened by the aspect of forlorn and decaying villages; wretched cabins, where a degraded race, of more than four millions, live a mere animal existence, in homes which it seems mockery to call a home; abodes of dreariness and discomfort, which a Northern laborer, or a European peasant would scorn to occupy for an hour. I have traversed England, France, Switzerland, Germany, and I do aver that in all those lands you see no habitations to compare with the "nigger cabins" at the South. These worn-out fields, these dilapidated dwellings, these poor, degraded white men and women, with no incentive to work, with all their energies paralyzed by those laws, framed exclusively for the benefit of the slaveholder, present one of the most oppressive aspects of gloom I have ever witnessed. The poor whites! Slavery seems almost more dreadful in its infliction upon them, than upon the blacks.

I do not wonder that the determined slave-holder is so very anxious to prevent these poor whites from learning how grievously they are defrauded. I do not wonder that, bowie-knife in hand, he watches the lips of the minister in the pulpit; that he tells the editor what he may say, and what he may not say; that he examines carefully every book before he will allow it to pass into the non-slaveholder's house; that he examines his list of newspapers and periodicals, and decides what he may take; and that he ransacks the mail, before it is distributed, lest his defrauded white brother should receive some chance pamphlet, which might pour upon his darkened vision some rays of the sun of liberty. What an awful, and undeniably truthful revelation of the oppression of the non-slaveholding whites at the

South, is contained in the following words, of George M. Weston.

"The non-slaveholding whites of the South, being not less than seven tenths of the whole number of whites, would seem to be entitled to some inquiry into their actual condition; and, especially, as they have no real political weight or consideration in the country, and little opportunity to speak for themselves. I have been for twenty years a reader of Southern newspapers, and a reader and hearer of Congressional debates, but in all that time I do not recollect ever to have seen or heard these non-slaveholding whites, referred to by Southern gentlemen as constituting any part of what they call '*the South.*'"

" When the rights of the South, or its wrongs, or its policy, or its interests, or its institutions are spoken of, reference is always intended to the rights, wrongs, policy, interests and institutions of the three hundred and forty-seven thousand slaveholders. Nobody gets into Congress from the South but by their direction; nobody speaks at Washington for any Southern interest except theirs.

"Yet there is at the South, quite another interest than theirs; embracing from two to three times as many white people, and who are entitled to the deepest sympathy and commiseration, in view of the material, intellectual and moral privations to which they have been subjected, the degradation to which they have already been reduced, and the still more fearful degradation to which they are threatened by the inevitable operation of existing causes and influences."

This poverty, ignorance, and debasement, are not merely sectional. They constitute a national calamity, an element of impoverishment, a running sore in the body-politic. The whole Union is weakened by it; and though a vastly greater calamity to the South than to the North, it is a calamity of such magnitude, that the whole nation is affected by it, and by the whole nation it must be deplored.

Listen to the testimony upon this point, for it is a vital one, of M. Tarver, of Missouri:

"The non-slaveholders," he says, in his report upon the Domestic Manufactures of the South and West, " possess generally but very small means; and the land which they possess is almost universally poor, and so sterile that a scanty subsistence is all that can be derived from its cultivation; and the more fertile soil, being in the possession of the slaveholders, must ever remain out of the power of those who have none. This state of things is a great drawback, and bears heavily upon, and depresses the moral energies of the poorer classes.

"The acquisition of a respectable position in the scale of wealth appears so difficult, that they decline the hopeless pursuit; and many of them settle down in habits of idleness, and become the almost passive subjects of all its consequences. And I lament to say, that I have observed of late years that an evident deterioration is taking place in this part of the population; the younger portion of it being less educated, less industrious, and in every point of view, less respectable than their ancestors."

One more witness I must bring upon the stand. It is William Gregg, of South-Carolina, who, in the following words, addressed the South-Carolina Institute in the year 1851.

"From the best estimates that I have been able to make, I put down the white people who ought to work and who do not, or who are so employed as to be wholly unproductive to the State, at one hundred and twenty-five thousand. Any man, who is an observer of things, could hardly pass through our country without being struck with the fact, that all the capital, enterprise, and intelligence, is employed in directing slave-labor; and the consequence is, that a large portion of our poor white people are suffered to while away an existence in a state but one step in advance of the Indian of the forest.

"We have collected, at Graniteville, about eight hundred people, and as likely a set of country-girls as may be found, but deplorably ignorant; three fourths of the adults not being able to read or to write their own names. It is indeed painful to be brought in contact with such ignorance and degradation. Shall we pass, unnoticed, the thousands of poor, ignorant, degraded white people among us, who, in this land of plenty, live in comparative nakedness and starvation! These may be startling statements, but they are, nevertheless, true; and if not believed in Charleston, the members of our Legislature, who have traversed the State, in electioneering campaigns, can attest the truth."

What a view does this give us of the kind of people South-Carolina is training up to support our republican institutions! Free and enlightened Americans, indeed! If we turn to the census of 1850, we find that the whole white population of the State of South-Carolina amounts to but two hundred and seventy-four thousand five hundred and sixty-three; hardly equal to one third of the city of New-York. And yet, of this feeble population, nearly a full half are in this state of brutal ignorance and beggary. What an awful gulf is this to whelm one of the States of the American Union! Poor South-Carolina! Must she, can she, our sister State, sink lower than this? There is hardly a county in the State of New-York which is not now superior to the whole State of South-Carolina in intelligence, in pecuniary resources, and in military power.

In view of similar results spreading their baleful influence over the once beautiful, prosperous, and glorious State of Virginia, Charles James Faulkner, in the Virginia House of Delegates, on the 20th of January, 1832, indignantly exclaimed:

"Does the slaveholder, while he is enjoying his slaves, reflect upon the deep injury and incalculable loss, which the possession of that property inflicts upon the true interests of the country? Slavery, it is admitted, is an evil; it is an institution which presses heavily against the best interests of the State. It banishes free white labor; it exterminates the mechanic, the artisan, the manufacturer. It deprives them of occupation. It deprives them of bread. It converts the energy of a community into indolence, its power into imbecility, its efficiency into weakness.

"Sir, being thus injurious, have we not a right to demand its extermination? Shall society suffer, that the slaveholder may continue to gather his *crop* of human flesh? What is mere pecuniary claim compared with the great interests of the common weal? Must the country languish, droop, die, that the slaveholder may flourish? Shall all the interests be subservient to one—all rights subordinate to those of the slaveholder? Has not the mechanic, have not the middle classes their rights —rights incompatible with the existence of slavery?"

It is thus that slavery drags the whites with the blacks down into the gulf of ignorance and penury. And it is impossible to rescue the poor white man without, at the same time, liberating the negro, whose Ethiopian skin is becoming so rapidly bleached by the infusion of the blood of his master. But the slaveholder seems to watch more carefully to keep the poor white man in subjection than he does to guard the slave. He knows that the slave is powerless, and, in case of an insurrection, can soon be shot down. But should the poor whites, at the South, begin to get their eyes open, and to claim their rights, they could not so easily be disposed of. H. R. Helper, of North-Carolina, has raised an earnest cry in behalf of the poor whites at the South; and did the world ever before hear such a clamor as that with which the single voice of Helper has been met by the slaveholders? He "touched the sore," and the whole civilized world has heard the scream the touch extorted.

I can not flatter myself that even this humble book will not be denounced as fanatical and incendiary. I fear that no bookseller at the South will dare to expose it upon his shelves, that no postmaster will dare to deliver it from the mail, and that no poor non-slaveholding whites will be permitted to read it. Gentlemen slaveholders, does it pay to practice all this vigilance and despotism, and to crush, actually, millions of your own white brethren, merely that you may be able to compel four millions of negroes to work without wages? It is an enormous price you pay in this world. And then think of the next!

CHAPTER VIII.

INSURRECTION: ITS MENACE AND PREVENTION.

Monday, Dec. 19. — At eight o'clock this morning, I took the cars, and, crossing the turbid flood of the Savannah, entered the State of South-Carolina. It was a warm, unclouded morning, and the sun, that wonderful beautifier, illumined the landscape, and, as we glided along over an undulating country, diversified with groves and streams and wide-expanded cotton fields, warmed and fertilized by a clime so genial, one could not but exclaim, What a favored region has God here provided for man! Nature seems to have lavished her gifts in richest abundance!

But what has man done to develop the resources thus placed at his disposal, and to embellish the garden thus given him to till and to enjoy? Vast regions are in solitude. Many fields are worn out by wasteful culture, and are abandoned. Old plantation-houses, deserted by their former inmates, are tumbling into ruins; and the negro cabins, hardly superior to ordinary pens for pigs, in their rottenness and desolation, harmonize with the whole aspect of decay. Occasionally we pass a mansion which presents some little air of gentility, but even the best of these residences have a lonely and unattractive aspect. But very little taste is expended in their external adornings. The " nigger cabins," in the vicinity, always look repulsive. These residences are widely scattered, remote from society, from schools, churches, shops, libraries, post-offices, and markets.

The cabins of the negroes, when regarded as homes for fathers and mothers, sons and daughters, are miserable indeed. I have not yet been so fortunate as to see one, in which there was a pane of glass, or in which there appeared to be more than a single room. I do not know but that there are plantations where the most tasteful cottages are reared for the negroes. I only speak of what I see along my line of travel. In all these "cabins," a hole cut through the wall, closed, occasionally, by a rough board shutter, affords the only entrance for light, except the door, and the chinks, often very wide and numerous, between the logs, boards or slabs which compose the building. I never see a plot of green grass, a yard, a shrub, or a flower. I have never yet passed through any country so entirely destitute of all picturesque, artistic beauty, *the work of man's hand,* as are our slaveholding States. And yet neither France, England, Switzerland nor Germany, can present such a diffusive display of taste as is gathered around the homes of the free States. The appreciation of the beautiful, attending the general expansion of intellectual culture, is spreading with marvelous rapidity, throughout the industrious and thrifty North. This difference can only be attributed to the difference in our social and political institutions. It is very rare that I see here any newspapers offered in the cars; there is no aspect of intelligence at the stopping-places, and the poor whites seem as totally destitute of ambition as are the slaves.

Let me mention one fact illustrative of this want of intelligence, and of interest in passing events. John Brown, for the attempt to emancipate the slaves by force, an attempt which, is inexcusable and can not be too severely condemned and deplored, was hung in Virginia, on the second day of December. It was an event which arrested, apparently, the attention of our whole country, North and South, to a degree almost unparalleled in the history of the nation. And yet, on Saturday evening, December the 18th, sixteen days after the execution of John Brown, a man in the cars, of ordinary respectable appearance, inquired of another, with a yawn: "Has Old Brown been hung yet?" "No!" was the reply. "I believe not. Some of them got away, I believe, but they have been caught again; but none have as yet been hung." At another time I heard two young men, over twenty years of age, disputing whether in writing 21, the 2 should come before or after the 1. This seems almost incredible. But when we remember that in benighted South-Carolina, there are scores of thousands who can neither read nor write their own names, such ignorance ceases to be remarkable.

In such a community, elevated so slightly in the scale of humanity; a community from which Northern newspapers are excluded, and where not even Southern newspapers can be read, it is easy for unprincipled men to rouse the masses to any violence. We no longer wonder that, in the capital of the State, a mob of three thousand could be collected to wreak the most inhuman barbarity upon a poor Irish stone-cutter, merely for expressing the opinion that the institution of Slavery operated to the prejudice of the poor whites. These wretched dupes are taught that those at the North, who are in favor of equal rights for all men, are their bitterest foes, that they wish to make them "no better than niggers," and that they would be glad to incite the slaves to rise and cut their throats! These unprincipled men do every thing in their power to prevent the poor whites from being undeceived. There is not another spot on the globe where the censorship of speech, and of the press, is so rigorous as it now is in the slaveholding States.

We have a glorious country, a common language, a common religion, and a Federal Constitution which, notwithstanding it contains some provisions that Washington deplored, and all good men must deplore, is, in my judgment, immeasurably better than that of which any other nation can boast. It has ever seemed to me that the framers of the Constitution must have been divinely aided, so wonderfully is that instrument calculated to elevate and ennoble. We have but to glance at our land, from the St. Lawrence to the Gulf, and from ocean to ocean, to see what our Constitution has accomplished in three quarters of a century, notwithstanding the crying oppression it has perpetuated in seemingly sustaining the slavery of four millions of our fellow-citizens. With Jefferson I call them "citizens;" for in every fiber of my soul I loathe and abhor the "Dred Scott Decision." I had rather have a mill-stone hanged about my neck, and be cast into the depths of the sea, than go to the bar of God with the blood of that "Decision," as I understand it, resting upon my soul.

We ought to be a happy and united people—united, not in the endeavor to rob four millions of our fallen brethren of their wages—to deprive them of all their social, civil and religious rights, and to doom them to perpetual ignorance and debasement, but united in the endeavor to elevate, instruct, and bless the whole population. We should take our feeble, unfortunate, degraded "brother," for it is with Jefferson that I call him "brother," by the hand, and encourage him to rear a cottage in the place of the "nigger cabin," into which our avarice has thrust him; we should establish schools for his instruction, and urge him to send his sons and daughters there; we should encourage him to subscribe for a newspaper, to purchase books, to plant shrubbery and flowers, and to rear the church, that most beautiful ornament, most efficient enlightener, and, in all respects, most inestimable benefactor of every population.

As I pencil these lines, my soul is saddened by the aspect of ignorance, oppression and debasement, which every where meet my eye. We are passing rapidly, in the cars, over the plains of South-Carolina. The sun shines brightly, and the landscape, save where deformed by man's work, is lovely. We are at this moment passing a vast cotton-field, spreading out over acres. It is beautiful, exceedingly beautiful. The snowy fibers are bursting from the bulbs, and the consciousness of the value of the product, adds to the attractiveness of the scene. There can be no agricultural employment more pleasant than the culture of the cotton. We need but the abolition of Slavery to whiten all these now abandoned fields with the gorgeous harvest, and to spread over all these lands, now being surrendered to desolation, farm-houses and villages, where comfort and intelligence shall combine their smiles.

There is a "gang of niggers" at work in this cotton-field, and that "gang" dispels every dream of beauty. Look at those coarse men, bare-headed, seemingly soulless, grinning like baboons! Look at those women! can it be that they are women! mothers! that any body ever *loved* them! Look at those girls! Are they daughters? Is it possible that they can have any maiden modesty! They seem, in the scale of being almost below the well-bred dog. Humanity, instructed in a Northern clime, sickens and weeps at the spectacle. They toil all day in the field, with no hope to cheer, perhaps with not even mind enough to be discontented. The iron has entered the soul, and the rust is there.

At night they go to their "nigger cabin." No neatly-spread table awaits them; no cheerful fireside, to invest with charms the chill, damp, frosty night; not even a tallow-candle to dispel the gloom. I have not yet seen in Louisiana, Alabama, Georgia or Carolina, a light in the evening in a negro hut. I should infer from the appearance of most of these negroes, that they are so debased that they would not even care for one. The father, at the close of the day's work, does not put the horse into the wagon, and take his wife and daughters to the prayer-meeting, the lyceum lecture, or to view the panorama, opening to the eye the wonders of the Hudson, the Nile, or the Rhine. Their souls are never stirred by the mysterious harmonies of the concert-room, or by the silvery tones and polished periods of Edward Everett, or by the irresistible humor of Irving or Dickens. History, literature, science are all alike excluded from their minds.

The "niggers" bake, in the ashes, their corn-bread; and, on the floor, or perhaps on wooden benches, eat their homely meal. And then, in the darkness, throwing themselves down on mats, or straw, as the case may be, males and females, young and old, together, without any change of their coarse, earth-soiled clothes, sleep, thank heaven, sweetly. For here God interposes, and in the slumbers of the night the slave is perhaps more happy than his master. Thus the monotony of the slave's dreary life passes from the cradle to the grave. Childhood, youth, manhood, old age, come and go, and there is no mental culture, no ambition, no hope, no progress. And this is called being "better off" than the laboring white man at the North.

In lands of freedom, in England, France, and with the free whites in America, the sons of labor are continually rising to the highest posts of emolument and honor. The coal-heaver's boy becomes Lord Chancellor, the peasant's son wins a coronet, and, from the log-house of the humblest tiller of the soil, the child of penury marches, with unfaltering step, to mansions of opulence or to the halls of a listening Senate.

No energetic man at the North, no matter how humbly born, need remain long in a log-house. He may boldly strike his way into the forest and tabernacle for a season, buoyant with hope in a mere camp. But this cabin he soons abandons to his cows or his pigs. The cheerful cottage or the stately mansion rises on the green lawn; and, year after year, he surrounds his home with new comforts and elegancies. His children, educated and refined, know nothing of the hardships through which their parents struggled. Blessed by the power of the true democratic doctrine, "A career open to talent, without regard to the distinctions of birth," they can achieve all that they have capacity to achieve, and every acquisition they make adds to their ability to make further acquisitions.

But with the slave, how different! "For me," he must say, "there is no hope. Morning, noon, and night, for days, weeks, months, and years, from the cradle to the grave, I must remain the same poor, ignorant, debased beast of burden. This miserable 'nigger-cabin' must be my only shelter until I die. The knowledge I crave I can never enjoy. My spirit, crushed and humiliated, forbids me from ever taking my position as a man. Had I the unconsciousness of a dog, my soul might be undisturbed. But I am doomed to the endless agony of feeling that I am a man, while I have to remain in the position of a beast."

A few years ago I dined with Mr. Frederick Douglass, whom all the world knows by reputation, as a slave of commingled Ethiopian and Caucasian blood, who fled from bondage, who wrote an account of the wrongs he had endured, in strains which caused the ears of England and America to tingle, and whose freedom was subsequently purchased by friends whom providence raised up for his protection. There were several gentlemen of distinction at the table, but Mr. Douglass, in my judgment, was second to none in social culture, in grasp of mind, in philosophical accuracy of thought. He is now an exile in England, having fled from his own country because he thinks, and his friends think, that the South is clamorous for his blood; and that under the Constitution there is not, even in the North, any power to afford him protection. In England he is received as a gentleman of distinction, and is welcomed to saloons where many of his vulgar persecutors could, by no means, gain admission.

There are thousands of slaves at the South, whose bosoms glow with the same indomitable love of liberty, which inspires the energies of Frederick Douglass. Perhaps two and a half millions are in such Egyptian darkness that they have but faint consciousness of their wrongs—born in slavery's subterranean mines, and delving there, without a ray of light, all their days, they know not that there is any gorgeous sun, or heaven-spread canopy, or lakes and streams and forests and flowers of freedom. Still there are *thousands* who have caught some faint gleams of this blessed light, and *they* hunger and thirst with "irrepressible" intenseness to see and enjoy more.

Many of them, through untold miseries, escape every year to Canada. How terrific the pressure must be which can induce them to accept the doom of such an exile? They must separate themselves forever from their friends, and can never visit them, or even hear from them again. There can be no interchange of loving letters. They leave all the associations of childhood; fields which their fathers have tilled; a warm and genial clime which they love, and go in poverty and friendlessness, with bloodhounds baying on their track, to a land of strangers, to icy winds and snow-clad fields, there to find employment *if they can;* perhaps to starve. But even all these sufferings, with liberty, they prefer to the doom of slavery. It is said that over forty thousand of the "citizens" of Thomas Jefferson have thus been driven from republican America by the oppression of our laws. The flag of Queen Victoria enfolds them protectingly in its embrace. England! with gushing hearts we thank thee! And must an American write this?

O God of our fathers! come to our deliverance.

Nothing can more impressively show the intolerable burden of slavery, than that so many thousands are willing to brave even such woes, that they may escape the scourgings which they are no longer able to bear. It is only when the flames of the burning steamer blister the skin, that one plunges into the turbid or icy waves, as the more tolerable death.

I counted the "gang" of slaves in the cotton-field we have just passed. All told, men and women, young and old, there were thirty-seven. At a little distance there was a row of cabins, called their "quarters;" and not far from these wretched shanties, a lonely, unattractive, unembellished two-story house, which is the abode of this moderate planter.

Now what is to be done with these poor people, or for them? Shall we try to induce them to run away? Nothing can be more unjustifiable or cruel. Where shall they run to?

and what shall they do when they get there? These poor plantation negroes are as ignorant and helpless as children. Oppression has burned out their eyes and cut the sinews of all their energies. It is far from improbable that their master, born to this inheritance, and regarding it by no means as it is regarded by those who breathe the air of liberty, is a *humane* man, in the ordinary acceptation of that term. He would scorn to treat his slaves with physical cruelty. He never speaks to them in harsh terms; he bears, with wonderful patience, their great faults; if they are sick, if he does not think they feign sickness, he has them cared for tenderly, as tenderly as any Northern gentleman would nurse a valuable horse, or a Devonshire cow. These slaves are worth fifteen hundred dollars perhaps, and their lives and health are not to be trifled with. It is by no means improbable that these poor slaves love their master, and lick the hand that at times caresses them. To advise them to run away is like advising the horse or the ox to abscond from the stable.

Shall we try to incite them to insurrection? Almost the whole united North shouts, as with a voice of thunder, no! ten thousand times ten thousand, no! Imagination can conceive of nothing more horrible than a servile insurrection. Plantations in flames, crops destroyed, men brained by the bludgeons of infuriate negroes, as Senator Sumner was beaten down by the bludgeon of Preston S. Brooks; mothers and daughters pursued by burly savages, powerful in lust and cunning in vengeance. The storm would be so awful that the whole energies of this nation would be instantly roused to quell it. We should inevitably lose all sympathy for the slave, in our abhorrence of the fiend-like outrages to which his ignorance and debasement would surely lead him. A servile insurrection could only result in misery to all, drenching the fields of the South alike in the blood of the whites and the blacks.

Even a *successful* insurrection, were it possible, as it is not, would only place the slave in a worse condition than now. He is as utterly incapable of framing a constitution, of organizing legislatures, of establishing courts, and of administering justice, as are the children in a primary school. Misery, bloodshed, and starvation would be the only harvest gathered on such a field. But such an event is impossible. What can four millions of ignorant, unarmed, unorganized slaves, humiliated and broken spirited by ages of oppression, accomplish in opposition to the power of the United States! It is true that these poor creatures, goaded to madness by some demoniac overseer, can, at any time, spread devastation, flames, and blood over a few plantations. There are small cities and solitary villages they can easily lay in ashes, and, for a few days, while a force is gathering to crush them, they can create inconceivable dismay and woe, and glut themselves with lust and vengeance. But then the bolt of the white man's wrath would fall, and they must inevitably perish.

These insurrections have ever been breaking out in all slaveholding countries, through all past times. They will continue to rise more and more frequently, and with constantly increasing power and desolation. The spirit of liberty is making wonderful advances; the mind of the world is expanding, and the dungeon of the bondman is more and more penetrated by these electric powers. The degraded slaves reason but little, have no intelligent consciousness of their weakness, and are easily roused by those fiery impulses, which they have in common with the lower animals. The secluded districts at the South, have much to fear from these sudden outbursts of frenzy, with which they are ever menaced. The unparalleled consternation which the trivial movement at Harper's Ferry created, reveals the conscious peril of the South more forcibly than words can tell. He who would incite the slave to insurrection rolls a wave of misery over the whites, and conducts the slave to inevitable death.

I am aware that there are those who say, that he who writes a word in condemnation of Slavery, or in expression of sympathy for the slave, exerts an influence, greater or less, should the slave chance to hear that word, to render him discontented with his lot, and thus increases the danger of insurrection. It will probably be said that this appeal, which is made not to the slaves, but to their oppressors, is insurrectionary in its character, and should be denounced as incendiary and fanatic. Just as well may you say that God ought not to reward freedom with blessings, lest the slave should see it and become dissatisfied with his chains.

I can only say, that it is my desire and my prayer to lead the South to that penitence and amendment which shall save them from insurrection. I have so strong an affection for multitudes of highly valued friends at the South, and have such a full conviction that nothing can save the South from a continued succession of servile revolts, but the recognition of the principle, that the "laborer is worthy of his hire," and that souls created in God's image should not be doomed, by human laws, to ignorance, that I am willing to expose my name to all the obloquy which, I am sure, that this appeal will draw down upon it, hoping that thus I may do something to avert, from every Southern State, the doom of Egypt and of Hayti. Our friends at the South do exceedingly misjudge us, when they think that we could rejoice over their calamity. There are bad men at the North as well as at the South. But I am sure that the desire, now so general and earnest at the North, that our land should be the land of Universal Liberty, is a desire founded in a friendly spirit to all men, and not in a hostile spirit to any section of our country.

The portents of danger, now menacing the South, to us are appalling. We, at a little distance, see them probably more distinctly than you do. The free negroes are being reënslaved, and the deadliest passions of rage and despair must rankle in their bosoms. The intelligent young slaves, from the hotels, and the streets, and the wharves of the populous cities, where they have acquired much energy and enlightenment, are being driven back to labor with the brutal, half-beastly gangs on the plantations; and the "*plantation nigger*" presents the lowest phase of humanity in the United States.

Maryland, Virginia, Kentucky, and Missouri, with marvelous rapidity, are driving their colored population down upon the plantations of the South. Many of these have more white than black blood in their veins. They are the children of sires who are regarded as men of property and standing; they are conscious of their lineage; their brothers and sisters, on their father's side, ride in the carriages and dance in the saloons of fashion. There are, among these maddened men, many of genius, like that which has given Frederick Douglass a name in two hemispheres; many with energies, like those which have rendered the name of Toussaint L'Ouverture illustrious throughout the world.

The young white men from the slave States, finding but little scope for their energies at home, are leaving, by thousands, for the North and the West. Among thirty millions of people, the terrific power of "fanaticism" will find many souls to fasten upon. That power is one which neither stake nor gibbet can intimidate. These "fanatics" will be continually rising under the delusion, that God has called them with a Mosaic call to lead the children of bondage into the Canaan of liberty. No earthly power can prevent this. There are more John Browns in the United States than the one recently hung at Harper's Ferry.

There are mercenary shop-keepers among us who care not what becomes of you or your children if they can only sell you goods. But the masses of the people at the North, humane and Christian, tremble in view of the doom which is approaching. "Apres nous," said Louis XV., "le deluge;" *after us, the deluge.* Those who entreated him to avert that deluge, by justice to the oppressed, were sent to the Oubliettes of the Bastile, or driven from the kingdom. The *deluge* came. We know something of its horrors. Will you, brethren of the South, bequeath such a deluge to your children? It can be averted only by justice and humanity. Am I your enemy, brethren, because I plead with you to spare your children this doom? It is easily done. All you have to do, is simply to substitute hired, for slave labor; pay your servants fair wages for their work.

As "love" is the fulfilling of the law, so is the simple recognition of the principle, that "the laborer is worthy of his hire," the panacea for Slavery. Adopt this sentiment of God's word, and there is no longer occasion to buy and sell your fellow-men in the shambles; no longer occasion to frame laws, dooming God's children to ignorance and degradation; and your emancipated brother has no longer any motive for insurrection. Churches may then rise in every village; free speech and a free press stimulate all minds, and the cloud, now so black and threatening, will be disarmed forever of its bolt.

CHAPTER IX.

THE REMEDY FOR SLAVERY: ITS SIMPLICITY AND SAFETY.

THERE is a general impression now, north of Mason and Dixon's line, that the whole South is in a blaze of fury against the people of the non-slaveholding States. And if we are to judge of public opinion at the South, by newspaper editorials, by speeches in convention, and by Congressional debates, it must be so. The following fact, explain it as any one may, is worthy of record. I have passed through Louisiana, Alabama, Georgia, and am now in the heart of South-Carolina, and yet I have not heard any where, in parlor, hotel, rail-car, or steamboat, one single unkind or intemperate word about the North. I have seen some editorials fiery enough to whelm the Union in flames. But the tone of conversation, wherever I have had an opportunity to listen to it, has been invariably mild, and not unfriendly. I had supposed that I should constantly hear the Yankees and the "Black Republicans" denounced in very unsavory epithets; but, thus far, I have not heard it in a single instance.

All day long we have been passing through the central portions of South-Carolina; continually encountering aspects of desolation and abandonment. We are now, as with my pencil I sketch these thoughts, passing one of those deserted plantations, of which we so often hear. The planter's mansion, windowless and doorless, presents the most gloomy picture of dilapidation. The forsaken cabins of the negroes, the old shed for the cotton-press, all the outbuildings pertaining to a plantation, have fallen into decay. The former proprietor has probably left these exhausted fields, and has wandered away, with his gangs of semi-savage slaves, to some distant lands, perhaps in Texas, where, in almost barbaric life, he raises cotton, that he may buy more slaves, and buys slaves, that he may raise more cotton. Every where, in the slave States, this aspect of premature decay is visible, even in the youngest and the freshest. It is comparatively but a few years since Alabama was reclaimed from the forest and the Indian. But listen to the testimony of the Hon. C. C. Clay, of Alabama, respecting the dilapidation which even now broods over his native State.

"I can show you," he says, "with sorrow, in the older portions of Alabama, and in my native county of Madison, the sad memorials of the artless and exhausting culture of cotton. Our small planters, after taking the cream off their lands, are going farther West and South, in search of other virgin lands, which they may and will despoil and impoverish in like manner. In 1825, Madison county cast about three thousand votes; now she can not cast exceeding two thousand three hundred.

"In traversing that county one will discover

numerous farm-houses, once the abode of industrious and intelligent freemen, now occupied by slaves, or tenantless, deserted and dilapidated. He will observe fields once fertile, now unfenced, abandoned, and covered with those evil harbingers—fox-tail and broom-sedge. He will see the moss growing on the mouldering walls of once thrifty villages, and will find 'one only master grasps the whole domain,' that once furnished happy homes for a dozen white families. Indeed, a country in its infancy, where fifty years ago scarce a forest tree had been felled by the axe of a pioneer, is already exhibiting the painful signs of senility and decay, apparent in Virginia and the Carolinas."

Where can we find any thing in New-York, Massachusetts, or Connecticut, to compare with this dismal picture? Massachusetts, occupying a region comparatively cold, bleak, and barren, is as a cultivated garden, in contrast with South-Carolina. Busy cities, lovely villages, industry, enterprise, picturesque villas and country seats, reared in the most approved style of modern architecture, every where meet the eye. The commercial metropolis of the State, Boston, with no cotton to export, and with a harbor often blocked with ice, has attained a population of one hundred and sixty-five thousand; and the libraries of Massachusetts alone, exceed those of all the slave States in the Union combined.

How speedily would free labor, with the dense population free labor secures, and with the schools, churches, and mechanic arts, which a dense population renders necessary, change the whole aspect of dilapidated South-Carolina, and of her little, antique commercial metropolis, Charleston. I am aware that some at the North think that the South are afraid to introduce the system of paying their servants wages, instead of holding them to work in bondage. It is a common saying with ignorant people at the North, that, should the planters emancipate their slaves from compulsory service, and hire them to work, the slaves would immediately "cut their master's throats."

I am sure that every man at the South will repel this cowardly suggestion with scorn. Are we afraid of the negroes? Must we, twenty-five millions of white people, keep four millions of poor, ignorant negroes tied, because we are afraid to untie them! We, with Saxon blood in our veins; we, with arms, intelligence, and organization; with an army, a navy, arsenals, and magazines; are we *afraid* that we can not manage four millions of negroes by the power of law? None would resent such a suggestion sooner than the South. "We no more fear our negroes," says a Southern representative in Congress, with a little pardonable exaggeration, "than the Northerners fear their sheep."

Then again the experiment has been fairly tried, on a scale sufficiently grand to be conclusive. When the slaves in the British West-Indies were emancipated, thirty years ago, though they were eight hundred thousand in number, and had long been suffering the severest kind of slavery, and, to say the least, were as unenlightened and debased as any which can be found in the United States, it is not known that a single drop of blood was shed, that a single blow was struck, or a single outrage committed. All remembrance of past wrongs seemed at once to be obliterated, and joy and gratitude were the only emotions cherished in the hearts of the emancipated.

Dr. Channing, writing of that event many years after it took place, says: "History contains no record more touching than the account of the religious, tender thankfulness which this vast boon awakened in the negro breast."

Prof. Hovey, who visited the island some years after the substitution of paid for compulsory labor, that he might investigate the results, testifies:

"The emancipated people, instead of becoming frantic with joy in the possession of their new rights and privileges, and rioting in the ebullition of ungoverned passions, retired from their places of devotion to their little tenements, without the commission of a single outrage, or the least disorderly conduct. The day was characterized by the stillness and solemnity of the Sabbath, rather than by the noise and tumult which usually, on such occasions, disgrace more intelligent and civilized communities."

There are few passages in history more eloquent and affecting than the narrative, by Thome and Kimball, of the manner in which the slaves, on the island of Antigua particularly, received their freedom. On this island there were thirty-four thousand five hundred slaves, and but two thousand whites. Though the *British Parliament* had decreed a system of apprenticeship, under which, as a greatly modified form of slavery, the negroes were to continue, in a certain degree, subject to their masters for six years, the planters rejected this preparatory course, and pronounced in favor of immediate emancipation. They decreed that upon the striking of the clock, at twelve o'clock at night, of the last day of July, ushering in the first of August, 1834, every slave should be instantaneously emancipated. In the twilight of that evening the slaves of Antigua were seen, in their best attire, hastening along the various footpaths of the plantations to their places of worship.

"The spacious chapel of St. John's," write Thome and Kimball, "was soon filled with the candidates for liberty. All was animation and eagerness. A mighty chorus of voices swelled the song of expectation and joy; and, as they united in prayer, the voice of the leader was drowned in the universal acclamation of thanksgiving, and praise, and blessing, and honor, and glory to God, who had come for their deliverance. In such exercises the evening was spent, until the hour of twelve o'clock approached. The presiding minister then proposed, that, when the clock on the cathedral should begin to strike, the whole congregation should fall on their knees, and receive the boon of freedom in silence.

"Accordingly, as the bell tolled its first note, the immense assembly fell prostrate on their knees. All was silence save the quivering, half-stifled breath of the struggling spirit. The slow notes of the clock fell upon the multitude. Peal on peal, peal on peal, rolled over the prostrate throng, in tones of angel-voices, thrilling among the desolate chords and weary heart-strings.

"Scarce had the clock sounded its last note, when the lightning flashed vividly around, and a loud peal of thunder roared along the sky, God's pillar of fire, and trump of jubilee. A moment of profoundest silence passing, then came the burst: they broke forth in prayer, they shouted, they sung glory hallelujah, they clapped their hands, leaped up, fell down, clasped each other in their free arms, cried, laughed, and went to and fro, tossing upwards their unfettered hands — but high above the whole, there was a mighty sound which ever and anon swelled up, it was the utterance, in broken negro dialect, of gratitude to God.

"After this gush of excitement had spent itself, and the congregation became calm, the religious exercises were resumed, and the remainder of the night was occupied in singing and prayer, in reading the Bible, and in addresses from the missionaries, explaining the nature of the freedom just received, and exhorting the free people to be industrious, steady, obedient to the laws; and to show themselves, in all things, worthy of the high boon which God had conferred upon them."

Such was the affectionate, religious gratitude which the gift of freedom awakened in the negro breast. The succeeding day, the first day of their emancipation, was passed as a sacred jubilee. There were no intemperate carousings, no mobs in city or country, but the rejoicing freemen met in their churches with their pastors, who, with martyr zeal, had suffered and toiled for them, and offered to God the incense of thankful hearts.

Such is the uncontradicted testimony upon this point. "I hazard nothing in saying," writes Prof. Hovey, who visited the island several years after the emancipation, "that the people of Antigua are as free from any apprehension of riot or insurrection, as is the most peaceful village in New-England. The militia, which was frequently on duty during slavery, and especially on the Christmas holidays, has not been called out, for the purpose of preserving the public peace, since the day of emancipation."

The fact is settled, conclusively settled, that there is no *danger* in substituting *free*, for *slave* labor. This experiment has been tried, not upon one island alone, where peculiar circumstances might favor its success, but in nineteen of the slave colonies of the British empire. The result, in *every instance*, was perfect safety. The *danger* lies only in compelling men to work without wages. They know that this is wrong and feel maddened by it. The smothered passions of the oppressed are ever struggling to break forth. Emancipation, and the guardianship of impartial law, dispel this danger. There is no longer any motive for insurrection, and all are equally interested in the public peace.

But it is said by some that negroes, mulattoes, quadroons, and quinteroons, will not work under the influence of wages; they can only be led to labor by compulsion. In emphatic reply to this, I would refer the reader to the petition of the Georgia planters to the Legislature of Georgia, to which I have referred. Alarmed by the industrial energy the colored people are manifesting, and the property they are acquiring, these men pray that the slaves may not be permitted to hire their own time, to own cabs, drays, and baggage-wagons, or to take contracts for work as mechanics.

On the levee at New-Orleans the negro gang, under a negro foreman, inspired by wages, would accomplish as much, and often, I am told by shipmasters, more than any gang of Irishmen or Germans. The poor fellows are now driven away from the city, where light would penetrate their darkened minds, to the gloom of the plantation, where no glimmer can tremble upon the eye-ball, and where they are indeed entombed.

It is said that the free negroes, in the slave States, are very indolent. Of course they are. They are almost as shiftless and miserable as the poor whites. Every effort is made, by the whites, to keep them degraded and ignorant and wretched. Who will have free negroes to work in the midst of his slaves? What slaveholder wishes to see an intelligent, industrious, and thrifty community of blacks in the vicinity of his bondmen, to show them the joys and the prosperity of liberty? No! to hold the slaves in bondage, it is necessary that those, belonging to their class, who chance to be free, should be kept so degraded that they may be pointed at as warnings—so that it may be said: "Slavery is much better for the negro than freedom."

A friend of mine, descending the Mississippi a few years ago, landed at Vicksburg, and called a colored man, whom he chanced to see, to take his trunk to the hotel. A young man, standing in the door of a store, cried out, "Here is a white man employing a free nigger;" and my friend informed me that he did not know but that he should be lynched for his inadvertence.

When the question of West-Indian emancipation was discussed in the British Parliament, it was said by many, and feared by more, that the moment the restraints of slavery were sundered, the negroes, spurning all control, would abandon the plantations and wander about in vice and beggary; that they, cherishing the idea that freedom from work is the choicest privilege of liberty, would resist every inducement to labor, and that universal misery would be the result.

But the experiment demonstrated that the negro loved his wife and child, and home and friends as well as the white man. He felt no disposition to abandon his family, now that he and they were cheered by freedom, and to wander away a fugitive and a vagabond. He had it now in his power to surround his home with new attractions; and he loved his wife and children better than even before, now he could press them to his bosom and call them his own.

It was found that upon all those estates where the slaves had been treated with any degree of humanity, they were eager to remain and work for their former masters for the most reasonable wages. The negro race is peculiarly an affectionate and clannish race. They love strongly their homes and the associations of place, and have but little disposition to wander.

When wages were substituted in the West-Indies, instead of the lash, the terms usually offered on the plantations were, the occupancy of the humble dwellings in which they had lived, the right of cultivating a small portion of ground, and eleven pence a day, which is about twenty-four cents of our money, for their work. The force of early attachments was so strong, that, on these terms, the freed slaves almost universally preferred to remain on the old plantations amidst scenes and associations endeared to them by time. As a general rule, no difficulty was found in cultivating the plantations; and it is universally testified, that under the healthly stimulus of wages, the emancipated slave has developed a degree of energy and skill which has surprised the planters.

Upon this all-important point the testimony of Prof. Hovey is as follows:

"As one of the greatest evils apprehended from emancipation, was, that the negroes would not work, I deem it of the utmost importance to say, that on those estates which have conciliating and judicious managers, which give job work in due proportion, there has been no falling off in labor. Such estates were never under better cultivation, and, in many cases, even with a diminished number of laborers, I was repeatedly assured, that should the crops be ever so great, they might be taken off without difficulty; and that no person would hesitate to commence any enterprise whatever, from an apprehension that laborers could not be obtained."

"It was formerly found almost impossible," Prof. Hovey continues, "to introduce any new utensils of husbandry. The negro would proceed in his old and indolent way, rejecting all innovations. For instance, a gentleman purchased a lot of wheel-barrows, with the intention of having the negroes use them, instead of baskets, to carry out manure. But they, not fancying these new notions, loaded the wheel-barrows, and mounted the whole upon their heads.

"Now, they eagerly avail themselves of all the facilities to expedite work. It is generally admitted, that they now perform as much work in forty-five hours, as they did formerly in all the week. No difference can be seen between them and white people in their eagerness to work for pay."

Mr. Buxton, an English gentleman, whose name is renowned in the annals of philanthropy, writes:

"Let it not be imagined that the negroes, who are not working on the estates of their old masters, are, on that account, idle. Even these are, in general, busily employed in cultivating their own grounds, in various descriptions of handicraft, in lime-burning or fishing, in benefiting themselves or the community, through some new but equally desired medium.

"Besides all this, stone walls are built, new houses erected, pastures cleaned, ditches dug, meadows drained, and numerous other operations effected, the whole of which, before emancipation, it would have been a folly even to attempt. The old notion," he continues, "that the negro is a lazy creature, who will do no work at all, except by compulsion, is now forever exploded."

One single fact precludes the necessity of all further testimony upon this point; it is the ever memorable fact stated by Mr. Gurney, that in the sixth year of freedom, after a fair trial of five years, the exports of sugar from Antigua, almost doubled the average of the last five years of Slavery.

"By whose hands," writes Mr. Gurney, "was this vast crop raised? By the hands of the lazy and impracticable race, as they have often been described, the negroes. And under what stimulus has the work been effected? Solely under that of moderate wages."

Thus is the fact established, that the emancipated slaves, under the influence of wages, may become industrious and thriving laborers. We want all these laborers. Not one of them can be spared.

In New-England, thousands of them are needed. How many an exhausted wife and mother would find her heart gladdened this day, and would offer those thanks to God, which bring tears to the eye, if a good, healthy colored girl or woman, could be sent to the family. I have, and have had for years, such a treasure. And were she in Liberia, I would pay a high price to bring her here. Many *hundred thousands* could this day be employed in the North, with wages varying from one dollar to two dollars a week. I can hardly conceive of a richer blessing which Heaven could confer upon the wives and mothers scattered over the rural districts of New-England, than to send them a supply of such servants. The North is in such an astonishing state of prosperity, that native Americans can generally do better than to go out to domestic service. We are almost entirely dependent upon Irish and German emigrants. And I have often been under the necessity of going to New-York, four hundred miles, and bringing such servants down to Maine.

In my own family we have had many excellent servants from the European emigrants; but we have never had servants more capable, more industrious, more devoted to our interests, feeling that they were one with us, than those of African descent. And we have never dreamed that our home would be more happy, or that our servants would love us more, or serve us more faithfully, if we owned them as property, and could threaten, in case of disobedience, to send them to the whipping-post, or the auction-block. Brethren of the South! I am not a fanatic, or your enemy, because I implore you to adopt this system, and thus do the only thing, which, by any possibility, can be done, to restore peace to our distracted country.

Surely I do not suppose that this change can be effected without encountering some friction, and meeting obstacles which wisdom and energy alone can surmount. But is there no friction now? Are there no obstacles now in our way? Does the car of Slavery run smoothly along its track? Upon the introduction of this change, there will doubtless be thousands of servants, maids in families, who desire no more freedom, so far as personal movement is concerned, than they have always had. Such a girl will say to her mistress, whom she loves and has always loved, or such a man will say to the indulgent master to whom he is so much attached, that he has no desire to leave his service, or to receive more than he has been receiving.

"If you will give me a home, and take care of me for the rest of my days, I will ask nothing more, and will serve you to the best of my ability."

If the master kiudly says: "In addition to this, I will give you a small sum each week, that you may have a little pocket-money," how entirely is the relationship changed, and how pleasant is the new aspect of affairs! There is no longer buying and selling—heart-crushing separations—slave-shambles! no more fugitive slave-laws, or blood-hounds; no more reënslaving the free, no more cruel enactments, to disgrace the nation and the age, dooming to eternal ignorance, immortal beings, created in the image of God. We then extend helping sympathy to our weaker brother, place the spelling-book and the Bible, those chiefest of all ennoblers, in his hand, and encourage him in the development of that whole nature, physical, moral and intellectual, with which God has endowed him, so that when, in his full redemption, he stands up proudly, and says: "Am I not a man and a brother?" we as proudly respond: "You are! You are!"

And now, brethren of the South, will you call me a fanatic and your enemy, because, deploring the wrongs inflicted upon our colored brother, and deploring the agitations which are making our country wretched, I entreat you, in your wisdom, to devise some measure by which you can substitute paid labor for compulsory labor? I only ask you to do that which we at the North do, which every enlightened nation on the globe does, excepting two hundred thousand slaveholders, all told, in the South.*

* Mr. H. R. Helper, in his *Impending Crisis*, after giving a tabular view of the number of slaveholders in the United States, according to the census of 1850, says:

"It thus appears that there are, in the United States, three hundred and forty-seven thousand five hundred and twenty-five slaveholders. But this appearance is deceptive. The actual number is certainly less than two hundred thousand. Prof. De Bow, the Superintendent of the Census, informs us, that 'the number includes slave-hirers,' and furthermore that 'where the party owns slaves, in different counties, or in different States, he will be entered more than once.' Now every Southerner, who has any practical knowledge of af-

We pay our servants for their work. When my washerwoman brings home my linen, I place the half or three fourths of a dollar, a dozen, in her hands, instead of threatening to whip her if she does not do the washing for me. And I find that the solid money accomplishes the purpose perfectly, far better than

fairs, must know, and does know, that every New-Year's day, like almost every other day, is desecrated in the South, by publicly hiring out slaves to a large number of non-slaveholders.

"With the statistics at our command, it is impossible for us to ascertain the exact number of slaveholders and non-slaveholding slave-hirers in the slave States; but we have data which will enable us to approach very near to the facts."

After a careful computation, which seems to be philosophically accurate, he says: "We find, as the result of our calculations, that the total number of actual slaveholders in the Union is precisely one hundred and eighty-six thousand five hundred and fifty-one, as follows:

Number of actual slaveholders in the United States,..............................186,551
Number entered more than once,.......... 2,000
Number of non-slaveholding slave-hirers,...158,974

Aggregate number according to De Bow,...347,525."

the gory whip could do. Now, why should not you do the same? All we ask of you is, that you should *pay your servants fair wages.* This is not a very hard requirement. And this settles the whole question. And nothing else can settle it.

It is in vain to hope that all the nations will abandon their principles, consolidated by the teachings of ages, that "*the laborer is worthy of his hire.*" It is vain to imagine that two hundred thousand slaveholders can convince the rest of the world that it is "wise, just, and beneficent" to compel men to work without wages, and consequently to be compelled to keep them in ignorance that they may not know how deeply they are wronged; to enact fugitive laws to catch them, when they endeavor to escape, and, as an essential part of the system, to have fathers and mothers, brothers and sisters, sold in the market, like horses and oxen. The religion of the world, the literature of the world, the political economy of the world, the conscience of the world, is against the slaveholder.

Now which is most reasonable to require, that in this conflict the millions of all enlightened nations should yield to two hundred thousand people who are unwilling to pay their servants wages, or that this handful of slaveholders should yield to the public sentiment of Christendom? Here is the point. All the rest of the world must yield, or the two hundred thousand slaveholders must yield, or there *must* be an eternal, " irrepressible conflict." There is not an intelligent man in Europe or America, who can deny that this is putting the question fairly.

Brethren of the South! this subject, as thus presented, does merit your calm and unimpassioned reflection. You are deceived when you imagine that a mere handful of noisy fanatics are puffing the bellows of senseless rage. It is a real *norther;* the whole force of the air of a hemisphere which is pressing down upon the Gulf of Slavery. Can this be arrested by resolutions and menaces? These menaces will bring those upon their knees who are so anxious to sell you goods, that they are willing to throw in their principles to boot—if they have any; and *they* will declare that the system of defrauding the laborer of his hire, and plucking out the eyes of the mind, and selling helpless girls to debauched men, is "wise, just, and beneficent." But such pitiable exhibitions of poor human nature, in its worst estate, are even more despised at the South than at the North.

It has never yet been my misfortune to meet personally with a man, at the North, in favor of the dissolution of this Union. I am aware that there are a few, a very few, of those who are usually called "ultra-abolitionists," and with whom the North is in but little sympathy, who have proclaimed this desire. They wish for disunion, for they know, and every intelligent man in our country knows, that disunion is abolition, and perhaps even bloody abolition; and *they* are willing to accept the evil of the blood, for the good of the abolition. But this number is so small that, extensive as is my acquaintance, I have never yet *met* with the man at the North who advocated disunion.

And here let me make a remark which I am sure will astonish my Northern brethren. On this trip to Cuba and the South, we had, in the steamer which took us from New-York to Havana and New-Orleans, one hundred and eighty passengers, who were mostly Cubans or Southerners. At New-Orleans I spent several days, and was introduced to a large number of friends; I crossed Lake Pontchartrain in a crowded steamer to Mobile; visited friends there; ascended the Alabama four hundred miles to Montgomery in one of the large river-boats, filled with Southern passengers; and thence, in rail-cars, passed through the heart of Alabama, Georgia, South-Carolina, North-Carolina, and Virginia, and during this whole route, in ocean-steamer, river-steamer, rail-car, parlor, and hotel, *I did not meet one single individual who advocated disunion!*

For aught I know, there may have been thousands in that region in favor of disunion, whom I did not meet; but I did not converse with a single one who advocated such views. On the contrary, I met many who spoke in tones of sadness of the bitterness of the strife, and who deplored the idea of any separation between the North and the South. As I perused the fierce denunciations in Congress, I was often led to inquire: "Where do these fiery spirits come from? and whom do they represent?"

CHAPTER X.

THE MOTIVE POWER OF WAGES.

ON this tour I have been continually meeting with incidents illustrative of the impolicy of attempting to compel people to work without wages. In conversing one day with a gentleman, a slaveholder, as we were ascending the Alabama river, he said:

"These servants are a heap of trouble. You often do not know what to do with them. I own four as good women as you can find in the State; and yet they almost worry my wife's life out. When I am away, they take the advantage, and are impertinent and willful. When I last went home, my wife had a long story of complaints. I called up Phillis, and said to her: 'Now, Phillis, I am going to sell you. You are saucy to your mistress. You are fit for nothing but a plantation nigger, and want a stern driver to make you know your place. I am going to sell you to one of those French planters down in Louisiana. I won't be plagued with you any more.'

"This frightened Phillis terribly, and she will be as good as honey for a few days; but then she will forget it all, and will be as bad as ever. I tell you these niggers are a heap of trouble. You don't want to take a woman and whip her. And that only makes her mad and worse. You can't dismiss her. And you don't exactly want to sell her. I tell you they are a heap of trouble."

This, certainly, is natural. She must have a wonderfully sweet disposition, who will work all her days as a kitchen scullion, from the cradle to the grave, kept in the state of most debasing ignorance, with no moral culture, and with no remuneration but such fare and dress as a scullion can find in a "nigger kitchen," and yet ever manifest an affectionate, faithful and docile spirit. Virtues and graces can not be bought at that price.

Another gentleman remarked to me, that people, in New-Orleans particularly, were getting very much in the habit of employing white servants, Irish and German, in their families, instead of slaves.

"It requires a great deal of knowledge of the negro character," said he, "to know how to manage these creatures. A lady rises in the morning, and finds that her cook is still in bed, affirming that she has a dreadful headache, or a severe attack of rheumatism. There are ten chances to one it is all a sham, and yet perhaps the humane lady will spend two or three days, nursing the artful deceiver. They are often very cunning. Perhaps the lady suspects that it is all sham, and yet is not certain that it is, and shrinks from the possibility of treating the servant cruelly. There are a great many such embarrassments. The best place for these poor creatures is on the plantation, where men who understand them can manage them."

THE MOTIVE POWER OF WAGES. 211

The payment of wages rectifies all this. If you will not work, neither shall you eat. A humane man, not thoroughly acquainted with negro tricks and cunning, who has one of these slaves, shamming sickness, does not know what to do with her. He does not wish to whip her; he does not wish to sell her. The only remedy is a general system of the substitution of wages, instead of compulsion. The hired servant at the North, will work when hardly able to work, lest both place and wages should be lost.

A kind Providence has thrown light upon our path, in reference to this great question, so that we need not go stumbling over a dark and unknown road. The experiment in the West-Indies has answered all our questions, and solved our difficulties. It was feared that the slaves, with no stimulus to work but the wages they might receive, would lie down and die in nakedness and starvation.

The Rev. Mr. Cadman, a clergyman, residing in the West-Indies, wrote some time after the emancipation: "The change for the better in the dress, demeanor, and welfare of the people is prodigious."

"A female proprietor," Mr. Gurney writes, "who had become embarrassed, was advised to sell off part of her property in small lots. The experiment answered her warmest expectations. The emancipated slaves in the neighborhood, bought up all the little freeholds, with extreme eagerness, made their payments faithfully, and lost no time in settling on the spots which they had purchased.

"They soon framed their houses, and brought their gardens into useful cultivation, with yams, bananas, plantains, pineapples and other fruits and vegetables, including plots of sugar-cane. In this way, Augusta and Liberta sprung up as if by magic. I visited several of the cottages, in company with the rector of the parish, and was surprised by the excellence of the buildings, as well as by the neat furniture, and cleanly little articles of daily use, which we found within. It was a scene of contentment and happiness, and I may certainly add, of industry.

"A wonderful scene we witnessed on Sabbath morning," continues the same writer. "The minister of the Baptist church was so obliging, as to invite us to hold our meeting with his flock. Such a flock we had not seen before, consisting of nearly three thousand black people, chiefly emancipated slaves, attired after their favorite custom, in neat white raiment, and most respectable and orderly in their demeanor and appearance. They appeared both to understand and appreciate the doctrines preached on the occasion. The congregation has greatly increased, both in numbers and in respectability, since the date of full freedom. They now entirely support a new mission, and are enlarging their chapel at an expense of five thousand dollars."

Volumes of authentic testimony might be quoted, corroborative of this point. In almost every particular, the condition of the slave has been meliorated by the substitution of wages for the lash. The marriage rite has become sacred. Home has been surrounded with new charms. Sabbath-schools are established, and churches sustained and thronged. The emancipated slave lives in a better dwelling than before; wears better clothing, eats better food; his children are better educated, and his family enjoy, to a vastly higher degree, all those influences which tend to purify and ennoble human character.

Though very much remains to be done in elevating a fallen race from the degradation of ages, the emancipated negro has proved that he takes much better care of himself, than his master took of him. No well-informed man will again say that the slave, if freed, will starve; that the stimulus of wages is not sufficient to incite him to work.

It is often said, that the master, if deprived of the unpaid service of the slave, will be reduced to beggary. But the master owns his land, his houses, his stock, and will own his crop, and can surely pay the laborer a suitable proportion of that crop for his services, in its culture. The Northern farmer can do this with his wheat and his hay. Why can not the Southern farmer do this with his sugar and his cotton? Here are the servants at his door all ready and eager to work for the most moderate wages. Surely there is no man more favorably situated than he for the accumulation of wealth.

The experiment in the West-Indies, proves that emancipation enriches, rather than impoverishes the master. The plantations, instead of falling into decay, have often flourished with new vigor. The planter has found that he can cultivate his estate *cheaper*, and make greater profits when his laborers are animated by wages, than when they are driven by the lash.

The Governor of Antigua, after six years of the experience of free, instead of slave-labor, says: "The pecuniary saving on many of the estates in Antigua, of free for slave-labor, is at least thirty per cent."

"The quantity of work," Mr. Gurney testifies, "obtained from a freeman, is far beyond the old task of the slave. In the laborious occupation of holing, the emancipated negroes perform double the work of the slave in a day. In road-making, the day's task under Slavery, was to break four barrels of stone. Now, by job-work, a weak hand will fill eight barrels, and a strong one from ten to twelve."

"I had rather," testifies a planter in Jamaica, "make sixty tierces of coffee under freedom, than even a hundred and twenty under Slavery. Such is the saving of expense, that I make a better profit by it. Nevertheless, I mean to make one hundred and twenty as heretofore."

"Real estate since emancipation, has so much risen in price," says the Governor of Antigua, "that at the lowest computation, the land, without a single slave upon it, is fully as valuable now, as it was, including all the slaves, before emancipation."

Robert Claxton, the Solicitor General of St.

Christopher's Island, testifies: "This property of mine, was worth only ten thousand dollars with the slaves upon it. Now, without a single slave, it is worth three times as much money. I would not sell it for thirty thousand dollars. This remarkable rise in the value of property, is by no means confined to particular estates."

It is needless to multiply this testimony, which could be done to almost any amount. I am aware that there are *rumors* floating, contradictory to these statements. But it will be observed that my appeal is not to *rumor*, whose reputation for veracity does not stand very high, but to the well-authenticated statements of reliable men.*

Now this is the change which the North wishes to see introduced to the South—the substitution of wages instead of compulsion, to induce labor. We wish to see the Southern

---

* The reader will find the above citations verified in the interesting narrative of Thome and Kimball, and of Prof. Hovey.

Legislatures introduce prompt and vigorous measures for the promotion of that system of free labor, which is adopted in almost every other portion of the civilized world. Their wisdom will suggest such laws, just and impartial, as may be required by the new order of things; laws based upon character, irrespective of color, binding equally upon all. The negroes should be offered fair wages for their work, with the liberty which this essentially involves, of seeking employment wherever they may best promote their own interests. There is no reason why the Southern gentlemen should not, as well as the Northern, pay the laborer who saws his wood, or ploughs his field, or gathers in his harvest. We only ask him to do that which every Englishman, and Frenchman, and Italian does; pay a fair day's wages for a fair day's work, and thus bring himself into harmony with the rest of the world. The result of such an emancipation is not problematical. The experiment has been tried in nineteen English slave colonies, upon a mass of eight hundred thousand slaves, and with entire success. Men are now incited to work by wages in India, China, Africa, Turkey, Russia, in the islands of the Pacific, among *all* tribes and nations. Why should two hundred thousand slaveholders persist in withholding wages from their servants, and thus place themselves in opposition to all the rest of the world, keep all these United States in turmoil, and endanger the most important experiment of liberty which was ever tried upon this globe? It is utterly inexcusable. It is a burning shame.

Gentlemen of the South, I repeat the asseveration, that I am not your enemy because I entreat you to introduce this change, and give our country peace. Thirty millions of people are kept in continual agitation, and bitterness and strife increase every hour of every day, menacing great national disasters, because you, brethren of the South, you, two hundred thousand only, a number hardly superior to that of two or three of the Wards in the single city of New-York, persist in refusing to pay your servants wages. And because I entreat you, in the name of humanity, to give us peace, will you denounce me as a fanatic, and an incendiary—offer a reward for my head—forbid your mails to carry this book, forbid the non-slaveholding whites at the South to read it, and order it to be burned at the hands of the common hangman! Believe me, gentlemen, such conduct does not reflect honor on your intelligence. This is not the way, in the nineteenth century, to meet the most momentous question, so far as our country is concerned, which that century has called up. You can not dam up the Gulf Stream, by dumping mud into the Gulf of Mexico.

The moral and religious influence of the substitution of free for slave labor in the West-Indies is worthy of especial notice.

"There is one point," writes Mr. Gurney, "which embraces and outweighs all the rest. I mean the diffusion of vital Christianity. I know that great apprehensions were entertained lest, on the cessation of Slavery, the negroes should break away at once from their masters and their ministers. But freedom has come; and, while their masters have not been forsaken, their religious teachers have become dearer to them than ever.

"Under the banner of liberty, the churches and meeting-houses have been enlarged and multiplied; the attendance has become regular and devout. The congregations have been, in many cases, more than doubled; above all, the conversion of souls, as we have reason to believe, has been going on to an extent never before known in these colonies. In a religious point of view, the wilderness, in many places has indeed begun to blossom as the rose."

Such has been the result of emancipation in the British West-Indies, and such is the change which every Christian patriot must desire to see introduced into the slaveholding States of our Union. The path of duty is henceforth a plain one, if there be only, in the hearts of those who have the *power*, a willingness to do their duty.

There is no embarrassment in the question, "What is to become of the slaves if we adopt the system of free labor?" We want every one of them. In the West-Indies, instead of sending any away, they are doing every thing in their power to induce more to come, and join the eight hundred thousand free laborers, who are now tilling those beautiful ocean isles. The United States, at this hour, need laborers, more than any thing else. We have millions of acres waiting for the plough of the cultivator. We have vast crops of corn, and hay, and sugar, and cotton, and wheat, which require the strong arms of industry, and the shout of free voices, welcoming the harvest home. The very moment that free labor is introduced we shall hear no more of the "nuisance" of having strong and docile men ready, for moderate wages, to till our soil. A kind Providence has spread them over the fertile fields of the country, instead of accumulating them in the cities. They are now just where they are needed. They understand just the

THE MOTIVE POWER OF WAGES. 223

work we wish them to do. They are acclimated. Their humble cabins are built, and they are so accustomed to them that, cheered by hope, they can endure them a little longer, until they can rear respectable homes. Schools may be established, and a race may thus be lifted from the lowest debasement to manhood.

Tell me not that this is fancy, speculation, a Utopian vision. It is fact. The thing has just been done before our eyes. All that we want is the *willing mind*. The Southern slaveholders, for they now wield the whole political power of the South, the non-slaveholders, the poor whites, having but little more influence in public affairs than the slaves themselves, should, in their Legislatures, by the enactment of laws, similar to those passed in the British Parliament, emancipate their slaves from compulsory labor, and substitute the system of free labor. The great agony will then be over, and we are at peace. Laws should unquestionably be passed adapted to the new order of things; laws prohibiting vagrancy, encouraging education, and stimulating every branch of industry; laws based upon character, not color; laws embracing equally Ethiopian and Caucasian. If the elective franchise be withheld, as it ought to be, from the negro, who is ignorant and debased, let it also be withheld from the white man, whether native or foreign born, who has sunk to the same level. If the negro acquire intelligence, property, moral worth, and thus prove himself a valuable citizen, let him enjoy the same political privileges which the Irishman, or the German, or the Yankee may enjoy under the same circumstances.

Let every man, irrespective of color, be offered fair wages for his work. Let every man, irrespective of color, be encouraged to make the most of himself he can, intellectually, morally, and physically. Let every man, irrespective of color, be permitted to seek such employment, and such employers, as may best promote his own interests. This is democracy, and we call ourselves democrats. I am a democrat, and mean to be a consistent one; a democrat in its true etymological sense.

The slaves, thus converted into freemen, with their long-lost rights restored, would have no motive for the destruction of property, or of life; but would at once become interested in the preservation of the public peace. As a general rule, they would remain in their present homes, and among the associates of their childhood, a free peasantry, cultivating their native fields, as hired laborers. Some few would purchase small farms for themselves. Gradually others would follow their example. The poor whites, incited by this change, and able to hire laborers, while they have been utterly unable to *buy* them, would see a new world of hope opening before them. Soon our whole Southern country would exhibit the aspect of cheerful and happy industry, which enlivens and blesses the North. The poor whites, now so debased, would rise to the position of proprietors, with hired servants, directed by their energies; the energies of a race now, doubtless, notwithstanding their debasement, superior to the colored race.

The colored man, inspired by the spirit of liberty, would develop new resources of body and of mind. His home would become attractive. His children, neatly dressed, would be gathered into Sabbath-school. The church bell would send its echoes over mountain and flowery savanna; and those sanctuaries of God, without which there can not exist an intelligent, virtuous, and industrious people, would diffuse their inestimable blessings over a rejoicing land. May God hasten the advent of this happy day. The man who, with a right spirit, prays and labors for this is neither a fanatic, nor an incendiary, nor an enemy of the South. Sure I am, that there are thousands of Southern wives and mothers whose hearts yearn for this blessing.

CHAPTER XI.

"THE IMPERTINENT INTERMEDDLING OF THE NORTH."

Tuesday, Dec. 20.—I have passed as cheerless a night in the cars as I remember ever to have experienced. It has been dark and rainy. At midnight we reached Wilmington in North-Carolina, two hundred and ninety miles from Augusta, Georgia. Crossing Cape Fear River in a boat, we took another train of cars for Petersburg, Virginia. But an accident befell our engine: we lost our right of way; and at six o'clock in the morning found that we had passed over but twenty-six miles.

I was much interested, during the night, in a gang of about one hundred young men, slaves, packed in the negro cars, who had been taken from Virginia, as I was informed, down to South-Carolina, to work upon a railroad. Some said that they had finished their work, and were being transported back again to their Virginia masters, of whom they had been hired. Others said that, through the considerate kindness of their owners and employers, they were returning home on a visit, that they might enjoy, with their friends, the Christmas holidays. I have received the impression, during my tour, that there is much of this kindness at the South. It was pleasant to observe that every body seemed interested in these poor slaves, and that they were always addressed kindly.

But is my eye evil, because, to me, this was a sad, sad spectacle? These poor young men have been absent from their homes, if a "nigger-cabin" can be called a home, perhaps six months or a year. All this time they have been hard at work, and yet their masters have received every dollar of their wages. Each man had a bundle upon his back, containing apparently a blanket and a lot of old shoes and clothes, tied up in a dirty sheet. In this compass was to be found all his earthly possessions; and even this was not his own. Perhaps some of them had children at home, but the poor father could carry the child no present, and least of all could he take to the little one a book to read. During all his absence he could receive no letter from home, and he could write none. And this is called kind treatment of our fellow-man! And we find men in the free North who will say that this system is "just, wise, and beneficent," and that the slave is in a better condition than the free laborer at the North! Young farmers and mechanics of the free States, with your purses, your homes, your education, your books, your newspapers, your lectures, your churches, and your freedom to seek and achieve your fortunes in any quarter of the globe, what say you to this sentiment? Are you willing to exchange places with some poor creature in this "gang"?

There were several overseers in charge of the

party. Most of the slaves were young men between eighteen and twenty-five. They were all comfortably clad in that coarse but warm and serviceable cloth, called "negro cloth." Some of the young men seemed reckless and a little merry, but I saw no indications of any thing like joyousness. The general aspect of the group was that of silence, patience, and weariness. Some countenances expressed positive sadness, and some few looked sullen and morose. But the general aspect was that of stolid indifference or hopelessness.

As I gazed upon this group, so melancholy in my contemplation, and reflected upon the unrefined, unintellectual, coarse, brutal life to which we doom them, I felt personally humiliated by the thought that we, a proud, powerful, intelligent, and professedly Christian people, should wield all the powers of our government to rivet their chains, and to darken their minds, and to check every effort these defrauded children of God may make for self-culture. And I blush for human nature, when I read the speeches of our Union-saving statesmen, so called, to find that, instead of urging the oppressor to break the heavy yoke, and thus to unite and save our land, they urge, with all the power of rhetoric, the Christian and the philanthropist, no longer to express any sympathy for the oppressed. Gentlemen, we can not heed your cry. We must, even if we perish at the stake for it, "Remember those that are in bonds as bound with them."

We, who plead the cause of the oppressed, enroll ourselves under the banner of Washington and Jefferson, Jay and Franklin. They have transmitted to us our watchwords. Speaking of this evil of slavery, Washington says:

"I can only say that there is not a man living who wishes more sincerely than I do to see the abolition of it."*

How earnest and emphatic the expression, "*there is not a man living.*" Mark also the phrase, the "*abolition*" of it. Washington does

* Letter to Robert Morris, April 12, 1786.

not ask merely for the restriction of slavery, merely for the melioration of its evils, but for "the abolition of it." He is for abolition. He is an abolitionist.

"There is," Washington continues, "only one proper and effectual plan by which it can be accomplished, and that is by legislative authority; *and this, as far as my suffrage will go, shall never be wanting.*"*

This is exactly what we desire. We wish you, gentlemen of the South, in your legislative assemblies to enact laws which shall substitute paid for slave-labor. We know that you can do this if you are only *willing* to do so. We know that it can be done with perfect safety; that it will be promotive of your own benefit, and of the welfare of our whole country. We feel that the power is with you entirely; and that all that we can do is to try to persuade you to exercise that power. As members of the human family, as fellow-countrymen, in-

* The same.

volved with you in the prosperity or the ruin of this great nation, we entreat you to do this, and thus to bring yourselves into harmony with the North and with the rest of Christendom.

Our Southern friends are so much in the habit of thinking of nothing but *Cotton*, that they are under the most extraordinary delusion in respect to its comparative value. As Cotton is their only child, it is not surprising that it should be regarded with undue partiality. With them there is the constant iteration of the old cry, "There's nothing like leather." This infatuation is too deeply rooted to be easily removed; and there are some apologies to be made for it, since the cotton-crop is, in reality, a very important one. By our last census it amounted, for the year 1850, to $78,264,628. This is more than half as much as the whole hay-crop of the North amounted to that year, which was $142,138,998. It is nearly three quarters as much as the Northern wheat-crop, which was $108,236,229. It is more than half as much as the Indian corn crop of the North, which amounted to $145,571,190.

Indeed the cotton-crop is a very important crop, so important that it deserves to be encouraged and prosecuted with new vigor. Free labor would speedily double the product, and add vastly to its importance as an element of national wealth. But my Southern friends must pardon me if I intimate to them—for, under the circumstances, it is my duty to do so—that in their talk about cotton they often remind us of the Chinese. I recently saw a map of China, in which the "Celestial Empire" composed nearly the whole of the globe. Far off in one corner there was a little dot, which represented the benighted island, where a few outside barbarians, called the English, lingered away a miserable existence. Still farther off there was another savage island where the barbaric Americans groped through their lives, in glooms, which no rays from the celestial empire ever irradiated.

Our Southern friends are deceived, ludicrously deceived, when they fancy that cotton is the mainspring of the world's mechanism; that cotton is the throbbing heart which impels the tide of life and energy to the remotest extremities of the body politic. England was a very respectable nation, even before the cotton-gin was invented. France, and Austria, and Spain, and Prussia were great powers, even when there were no "niggers" growing cotton in Georgia. Should all the slave States suddenly slide down into the Gulf, there would still be twenty-five millions of people in the free States, whom that calamity would not annihilate; who would still contrive to eat and drink, build houses, take merry sleigh-rides, and marry, and be given in marriage.

The Southern delusion with regard to the sovereignty of cotton is so extraordinary, that we are continually meeting it in utterances which have never been surpassed by Esquimaux or Chinaman. A Southern Representative in Congress, only this last week, stated in the Hall of our National Legislature, that the cotton-crop of Georgia alone, for any one year, was sufficient to buy up the whole State of Pennsylvania!

Why, the products of the mining and mechanic arts alone, in the single State of Pennsylvania, in the year 1850, according to our last census, amounted to *twice* as much as *the whole cotton-crop of all the slave States in the Union put together.* Here are the figures:

Products of mines and mechanic arts in Pennsylvania, for 1850,	$155,044,910
Cotton-crop of all the Slave States,	78,264,928
Balance in favor of Pennsylvania,	$76,779,982

Indeed, all the staple agricultural products, of all the slave States, including cotton, tobacco, rice, hay, hemp and sugar, amounted, for the year 1850, to but $138,605,723. Thus, the single State of Pennsylvania, from the annual products of her mines and manufactures alone, could buy up the whole cotton-crop of all the Southern States, together with all their other staple agricultural products, and yet have the pretty little sum of more than $16,000,000 left in her purse. And, yet a Southern Member of Congress actually thinks that Pennsylvania is a poor, outside barbarian, whose very existence is dependent upon the cotton raised by Southern "niggers."

Pennsylvania can show property to the amount of $729,144,998. She could buy up to-day, all the cities, villages, railroads, cabins, planters' houses, lands and "niggers" of Georgia, and still have a well-invested capital, amounting to $393,719,284. With this surplus capital, she could buy up still another State like Georgia, "niggers" and all, and then have $58,293,570 left in her purse. Here are the figures:

Real and personal property of Pennsylvania, in 1850,	$729,144,998
Real and personal property of Georgia, including slaves,	335,425,714

It is of no use to get angry with the multiplication table, or with Euclid's problems. Here are the facts. Wise men will ponder them. They will inquire into the cause of this amazing difference between two sister States. Is

Pennsylvania larger than Georgia? No! Has she a more genial climate? No! Better soil? No! What makes the difference? *One is blest with free labor, and the other is cursed with slave labor !* That is all.

We are singing a great song of liberty: we, a choir of thirty millions. You, a little band of slaveholders, have come in with the discordant strains of slavery. We ask you to sing in harmony with us. But you refuse, and insist that we shall change our concert-pitch, and strike up a strain which we do not know, can never learn, and absolutely abhor. And you threaten that if we, the millions, do not obey you, the thousands, you will leave the orchestra and break up the choir. Gentlemen! do you really think that we shall yield!

It will not be a creditable story, in this age, to go out to the world, that the Southern States of the American Republic abandoned the Confederacy, because the Northern States would not help them compel their servants to work without wages. Men, thus dishonoring themselves, will not find a welcome at any table, where gentlemen do congregate, in Christendom.

But, our Southern friends ask, "What is it to you, at the North, whether we pay our servants or not? We have a right to do what we will with our own. We deny that we ask any help of you in the management of our servants. We can take care of them ourselves. All we ask of you is that you will let us alone, and not impertinently meddle with that which is no concern of yours."

Have I put it fairly? Now will you listen to my reply! Here is a fugitive slave, rushing across the frontier, panting, bleeding, exhausted. The baying bloodhounds are on his track, and the shouts of men are heard closely following, with their guns shotted and primed, hounding on the dogs.

You shout to us, in our free fields and cities, to help your bloodhounds catch the fugitive. The man has committed no crime. He seeks only liberty. He is fleeing only from oppression, such oppression as *we* would not endure for an hour. Imperiously you shout to us to join your bloodhounds in the pursuit. You call upon Cincinnati and Philadelphia and Worcester and Boston to change themselves into dogs to help you catch your negroes!

Gentlemen! is this what you call "asking no help of us"? Is this what you mean, when you say: "All that we ask of you is, that you will let us alone, and not impertinently intermeddle with that which is no concern of yours"?

When we hesitate to clutch the poor fugitive, and to join with the dogs in dragging him down; when we find our sympathies instinctively arising against the bloodhounds, and in favor of the man, you point us to a cautiously worded phrase in the Constitution, about "persons held to service," and aver, that by that clause we are bound to help your dogs; that it is one of the solemn compromises of the Constitution that we shall "help you" catch your slaves, and rivet again upon their wrists the broken manacles, and send them back again to eternal bondage. And when, in the anguish of our hearts, we declare that we do not see how we can perpetrate this great crime —that to our enlightened consciences, it does seem the very meanest and wickedest thing a man can do, you tell us in the harshest tones of Saxon utterance, that we are Fanatics, and Incendiaries, and Traitors.

Many a pang of anguish was felt a few years ago in the city of Boston, and the whole State of Massachusetts blushed crimson with shame, when poor Burns, a helpless, innocent, Christian man, whose only crime was, that he loved liberty, was seized by the whole military power of the city, and, guarded by battalions of infantry, cavalry and artillery, was dragged back again to bondage. There is an amount of oppression which will drive a wise man mad. Boston narrowly escaped that doom. At many a family altar that night, tears flowed freely, and voices, inarticulate with emotion, breathed agonizing prayers.

It was, indeed, a dreadful spectacle! Those who beheld will not forget it till their dying day. As poor Burns was borne along in that sad, funeral procession, almost beneath the shadow of the monument on Bunker's hill, tears dropped from his eyes, bedewing the soil which our fathers crimsoned with their blood, in support of the principle that: "All men are endowed by their Creator with certain inalienable rights; that among these are life, liberty, and the pursuit of happiness."

And now, will you, brethren of the South, still ask: "What has the North to do with Slavery? Will you denounce us as impertinent intermeddlers, because we *entreat you* to substitute free labor for slave labor, and thus give peace to our country, and save us from this shame and woe?

You can not compel men to work without wages, unless you keep them in the most profound ignorance. They must neither be permitted to read nor to write. They must learn no philosophy, no science. The Bible above all things must be excluded from their minds. The slave must be kept down in the dungeons of mental gloom, far from the light of day. Samson's eyes must be plucked out before he can be forced to grind in the mill of the Philistines. Now we are one nation. The Constitutional provision to which you so often refer us, implicates us all alike in the institution of Slavery. We feel degraded in our own eyes, and know that we are degraded in the eyes of the whole civilized world, by trying to keep four millions of people in the condition of brutes. The voice of nature and of inspiration alike declares, that every man should make the most of himself, developing and ennobling all the powers which God has conferred upon him.

Suppose that every colored child, as soon as born, were taken into the arms of its "owner," and a red-hot needle thrust into its eyes, that it might be blinded forever. That is just what we do to the *eyes of the mind* of more than four millions of people. Not *you*, but *we*, for we have entered into a partnership with you in this thing. I can not conceive of a more awful crime than this. And this crime we must continue to perpetrate, if we are determined never to pay these people wages. We must *blind* them. Then they are helpless and groping; can neither resist nor strike. May I not, then, brethren, plead with you to adopt the system, that the "laborer is worty of his hire," a system which all the rest of enlightened Christendom has adopted; a system which renders this blinding process no longer necessary? Ought you not to be willing to make so slight a sacrifice as this, for the peace of your country? If not, can you dream that thirty millions of people will pass over to your views; when, should they do so, all the rest of the civilized world would cry shame! shame! shame!

CHAPTER XII.

SOUTHERN AGGRESSION — A NORTHERN VIEW.

WE hear much, from our Southern friends, respecting the aggression of the North upon their rights. Let me exhibit this subject of aggression as it presents itself to the eye from my point of view.

1. The effort at the South, to compel their servants to work without wages, throws obstructions into our paths at the North, in almost whatever direction we may attempt to move. The slaveholder demands permission to bring his slaves into our States, and hold them there, as a visitor, so long as it may be convenient for him to do so. And he commands us so to amend and frame our laws, as to enable him to grasp his slave firmly, and extort from

him unpaid labor. So far as he is concerned, he demands permission to bring into our States the slave code of the slave States, a code utterly abhorrent to all our feelings and principles, and which is in antagonism with the whole spirit of our laws. And because we refuse to do that which a man would be insane to demand of England or of France, we are denounced in the severest terms language can afford.

2. If a Northern gentleman wishes to journey South, with a colored servant, to whom he pays wages, you seize that servant, and throw him into jail and keep him there until his employer leaves the State. If we send a ship to the South, and have in our employ a colored sailor, or cook, you seize that man, drag him from our service, and shut him up in prison, until our ship weighs anchor and departs. Thus you claim the privilege of carrying your institution of Slavery to the North, but refuse us the right of carrying our institution of freedom to the South. And how inglorious the reason you as-

sign. "If the Southern slaves," you say, "see that Northern servants are paid for their work, they will be discontented in working without wages, and will want pay also!"

3. Annoyed by having our hired servants thus torn from us, and thrust into jail, Massachusetts sends one of her most distinguished citizens, the Hon. Mr. Hoar, as an ambassador to the State of South-Carolina, to inquire, in a friendly spirit, if an evil of such magnitude may not, in some way, be redressed. He goes as a man of peace, with no retinue, with no menace; an unarmed ambassador, accompanied by his daughter.

Instantly this ambassador, with barbarity almost unparalleled in the annals of nations, is met with the grossest insults. A mob of gentlemen, of property and standing, leading on the "poor whites," surround him with hootings and yellings. He is threatened with tar and feathers, and only saves himself from the horrors of lynch law by a precipitate escape. There is not a nation in Europe which would not regard such an outrage as an occasion for war.

4. And now comes another struggle. You avow a new principle, which, in language not very classical, you call "Squatter Sovereignty;" that is, that the emigrants who first enter a territory shall decide, by a majority of votes, what institutions they will have, whether those of freedom or Slavery. Kansas is now the prize to be struggled for. The Missouri Compromise made it ours. To introduce this principle you repeal the Missouri Compromise. We are thus defrauded of Kansas, and must try to win it again by the energies of emigration. As slaveholding Missouri was the only State in the Union which bordered this territory, you affirmed, and we feared, that you could easily pour in such a tide of emigration as would doom these wide realms to Slavery; and that then you would sweep, with the disastrous flood of unpaid labor, the whole free territory to the Pacific.

5. And now came another act in this strange

drama, in this conflict so truly "irrepressible." The free States, roused by the great fraud of which they had been the victims, sent their sons and daughters, in multitudinous troops, from all the hills and valleys of the North and the West, to rescue, by the peaceful energies of the ballot-box, these lands from their impending doom. Slavery, also aroused, pealed forth her cry, and from Missouri, South-Carolina, Georgia and all the South, hosts were mustered to hasten to the arena, where you had declared, gentlemen, notwithstanding all our remonstrances, that the land we once had purchased by compromise, should no longer be ours, but should again be contended for in the strife of emigration.

6. And now occurred, in this dark and stormy tragedy, perhaps the most atrocious scene of outrage ever witnessed in a civilized land. It was soon evident that the sons of freedom were outnumbering the champions of Slavery. The appointed day was at hand for the inhabitants of the territory, the advocates

of Slavery and the friends of freedom, to meet at the polls, and, by a majority vote, decide whether freedom or Slavery should be the law of the land, and organize the government accordingly. There could be no doubt as to the result. Freedom outnumbered Slavery two to one.

In this crisis, Slavery rallied her legions, wild and savage men, from the dregs of the populace of Missouri, inflamed them with whisky, armed them with rifles, bowie-knives, bludgeons, and revolvers, and marched them across the borders of Missouri into the Territory of Kansas. These men, under the guidance of a slaveholder, a former Vice-President of the United States, took possession of the polls, overpowered and drove away the friends of freedom, deposited their own ballots in any number they chose, went through the farce of counting them; and then announced that, by an overwhelming majority of votes, *Slavery was declared to be the law of the land.*

They then organized the government by

electing a Legislature of slaveholders, who were to frame laws in accordance with these proceedings. To protect this Legislature from the indignation of an outraged people, this armed mob convened them in a small town near the borders of Missouri, where the "border ruffians" of that State could guide their movements, and watch over them. This Legislature met, and enacted a code of laws, which would have disgraced a tribe of savages. They put the strongest prohibition upon freedom of speech, and the press; dooming any one to death who should venture to write or speak a word against Slavery, or in behalf of liberty.

This armed invasion from Missouri was estimated to consist of from five to seven thousand men. As they were preparing for their march, one of their leaders thus addressed them:

"To those who have qualms of conscience as to violating laws, State or national, the time has come when such impositions must be disregarded, as your rights and property are in danger. I advise you one and all to enter every election district in Kansas, and vote at the point of the bowie-knife and revolver. Neither give nor take quarter, as our case demands it. It is enough that the slaveholding interest wills it, from which there is no appeal."

The march of these invaders resembled the movements of an army. They went with artillery, and tents, and mounted horsemen; with bands of martial music, and banners, and wagons of ammunition. They moved so strong in numbers that all resistance in the infant territory was unavailing; and thus Kansas was conquered and subjugated by the slave power, and all the most sacred rights of American freemen were trampled in the dust.

The army returned in triumph to Missouri, and entered the city of Independence. The *Squatter Sovereign*, a newspaper published in that region, devoted to the slaveholding interests, thus describes the scene of their return.

"They were preceded by the Westport and Independence brass bands. They came in at the west side of the public square, and proceeded entirely around it, cheering us with fine music and good news. Immediately following the bands were about two hundred horsemen, in regular order. Following these were one hundred and fifty wagons and carriages. *They report that not a single anti-slavery man will be in the Legislature of Kansas.* We have made a clean sweep."

7. And now comes another view, if possible still more revolting, in this panorama of "aggression." The Free-State men of Kansas, composing a vast majority of the population, resolved that they would not submit to such outrages, and that they would not recognize as law the exactions of this Legislature, thus created. They met in convention, and passed the following resolution :

"*Resolved*, That the body of men who, for the last two months, have been passing laws for the people of our territory, moved, counseled, and dictated to by the demagogues of Missouri, are to us a foreign body, representing only the lawless invaders who elected them, and not the people of the territory; that we repudiate their action as the monstrous consummation of an act of violence, usurpation, and fraud, unparalleled in the history of the Union."

"You shall obey our Legislature," shouted the voice of Slavery. They rang the tocsin, summoned their hosts, and again, in battle array, invaded the territory with threats of fire and blood. From all parts of the South, armed bands marched to swell the numbers, and increase the terror of this invading host. The Free-State men grasped their arms, and from all parts of the North aid was sent to our sons, brothers, and friends, who had emigrated to Kansas, in their struggle for their rights.

While matters were in this state, the President of the United States, in reply to a prayer from the people of Kansas for his protection, issued a proclamation, declaring that the Legislature created by the border ruffians of Missouri, was to be recognized as the legitimate Legislature of Kansas, and that its laws were to be binding upon the people. At the same time he dispatched officers to Kansas, empowering them to employ the whole strength of the governmental arm of the United States, in forcing upon the people of Kansas, the laws enacted by a Legislature created by a Missouri mob.

By this act of the United States in adopting these laws, any one who opposed them could be arraigned for treason against the United States. And in our National Senate, these men, who were defending their dearest rights, and who would have merited the scorn of the world, had they succumbed to such oppression, were stigmatized as "rioters and rebels." Encouraged by this support, the Missouri ruffian Legislature, passed an act declaring that no man should be permitted to vote in Kansas, who would not first take an oath that he approved of the most obnoxious acts of this ruffian Legislature. And, that they might obtain as many votes as they pleased from Missouri, they passed another act declaring that any man might vote, taking this oath, who would pay a tax of one dollar, and who would declare that at that hour he resided in Kansas.

Gentlemen of the South, how can you say one word about John Brown! A poor half-crazed, fanatical old man, with a single score of followers, black and white, stole by night into the State of Virginia, and tried to run off a few slaves. The scheme, in all its aspects, was as wild as monomaniac ever attempted. The poor old man was taken and hung for his crime. The North, with perfect ease, could have sent an army of one hundred thousand men for his rescue. But the North did not lift a finger. Almost universally it condemned the act as a crime, and acquiesced in the punishment. But any development of heroism and sincerity and entire unselfishness we can not but admire. No one can doubt that John Brown, though he was doing wrong, *thought* that he was doing right. Not a pang of compunction visited his soul. He ascended the scaffold as serenely as ever martyr was led to the stake. His unselfishness and his heroism we appreciate as noble, while his *act* we condemn. You, surely, are capable of understanding that distinction. And yet the world has been deafened with the clamor you have raised, about the crazy attempt of poor old John Brown, while all the unutterable outrages perpetrated by Slavery in Kansas, you do not seem to think even require an apology.

> O wad some power the giftie gie us,
> To see oursel's as others see us;
> It wad frae monie a blunder frae us,
> And foolish notion;
> What airs in dress an' gait wad lea'e us,
> And ev'n Devotion.

8. But we must still pass on, contemplating picture after picture in this career of crime. The friends of freedom in Washington, to rescue the territory of Kansas from civil war, introduced a bill into the Senate, through the Hon. Wm. H. Seward, providing for the immediate admission of Kansas into the Union, as a

free State, in accordance with the known wish of an overwhelming majority of its inhabitants. The Hon. Charles Sumner, Senator from Massachusetts, made a speech in advocacy of this measure; a speech in which he told the tale of Kansas outrage, in terms of fidelity, which caused the ear of Slavery to tingle. There was not one word in this speech transcending the allowed limits of Parliamentary debate. The proof of this is indubitable; for no one called him to order. "It was a speech," says a venerable statesman, " exceeding not one hair's breadth any line of truth or duty."

Slavery exasperated, and emboldened by having crushed freedom of speech and of the press in Kansas, determined also to palsy every free tongue in the Senate of the United States. The arguments of the Massachusetts Senator could not be refuted. He must be silenced with the bludgeon.

The Hon. Preston S. Brooks, a member of the House of Representatives from South-Carolina, armed with a revolver and a bludgeon, and accompanied by a confederate, that there might be two to one, should the Senator prove successful in resistance, stole into the Senate Chamber, where their victim, all unsuspicious of danger, was calmly writing at his desk, his limbs being so entangled beneath the desk that he could not easily rise. Mr. Brooks, a man of more than six feet in stature, and of powerful sinews, cautiously drew near, and with a gutta-percha bludgeon, so tough and heavy that it truly might be called an instrument of death, dealt blow after blow, with all the energy of his herculean arm, upon the brow of the Senator. Taken all at unawares, and stunned by this fearful, brutal onslaught, Mr. Sumner in vain attempted to rise. But the assailant, as with a frenzied arm, dealt, without an instant's intermission, these crushing, lacerating, mangling blows, until the scalp was peeled from the bone; the brain was paralyzed, and the blood, gushing from his wounds, saturated his clothes, and dripped in pools upon the floor, and the Senator dropped, senseless and apparently lifeless, from his seat.

The Hon. Edwin D. Morgan, of New-York, who chanced to be in the Senate Chamber at this time, gives the following description of this scene:

"It was by the merest accident I was present in the great slaughter-house of Washington. Business called me there, and while I was in conversation with one of the representatives of the press from New-York, I heard the first and second blows upon Senator Sumner's head. Instantly my friend and myself pressed forward towards the scene of conflict. It was the impulse of our nature, of every true man's nature, and no credit is due to us; because there is no *man* who would not have done the same. I saw, from the instant that I started from the opposite side of the Senate Chamber, that these blows were given on a defenseless man. These blows were given with all the power that a man six feet three inches high could inflict on a man seated at his desk, without the capability of rising.

"During the brief time that I was passing

from one end of the Senate Chamber to the other, fifteen or twenty blows were given with as much rapidity as the cane could descend in the hand of an active and powerful man. My friend, his name was Murray, caught the villain, Brooks, by the arm. Almost at the same instant my good fortune brought me to place myself between the beaten Senator and the assassin. I caught Mr. Sumner and saved him from actually falling on the floor. I laid him on the floor, sustaining him with my arm, and this coat, which I now wear, was saturated with his poor blood."

Will it be said that this was but an individual act of violence, and that slavery is not to be held responsible for it? There is not an intelligent man in the United States who will make any such assertion. Slavery, with almost a united voice, applauded the deed, appropriated it to herself, and gloried in the shame as "gallant" and "chivalrous." Slaveholding Senators rose in the Senate Chamber, and awarded praise to the assailant. The people of the slaveholding States, met in immense assemblages, passed resolutions in honor of the act, invited the perpetrator to triumphal fetes, and rewarded him with rich services of plate. His own native State exhausts its ingenuity in devising honors for Preston S. Brooks. With all pompous formalities they send him a new bludgeon, a substitute for the one which he shivered over the brow of one of the noblest sons of New-England; and on that bludgeon they inscribe the words, "Hit him again!"

Gentlemen of the South, can you, without a blush, utter one word of complaint about Northern sympathy for poor John Brown in his attempt, through a mistaken delusion, to help the oppressed!

Perhaps some may think it incredible that the South could have approved of the murderous assault of Preston S. Brooks. It is necessary then to adduce evidence. I do it with repugnance. The Richmond *Whig*, of Virginia, commenting upon this transaction, says:

"It will be seen by telegraph, that Mr.

Brooks, of South-Carolina, after the adjournment of the Senate, on yesterday, administered to Senator Sumner, the notorious and foul-mouthed abolitionist from Massachusetts, an effectual caning. We are rejoiced at this. The only regret we feel is, that Mr. Brooks did not employ a horse-whip or a cowhide upon his slanderous back, instead of a cane. We trust that the ball may be kept in motion. Seward and others should catch it next."

The *South-Side Democrat*, of Virginia, says: "The telegraph has recently announced no information more grateful to our feelings than the classical caning which this outrageous abolitionist received on Thursday, at the hands of the chivalrous Brooks, of South-Carolina."

The *Petersburg Intelligencer*, Virginia, says: "We are exceedingly sorry that Mr. Brooks dirtied his cane by laying it across the shoulders of the blackguard Sumner. We regret that he did so, not because Sumner got a lick amiss, not because he was not entitled to all he got and more besides, but because the nasty scamp and his co-scamps will make capital for their foul cause out of the affair. They will raise a howl, which will split the public ear, about the violation of the privileges of debate, Southern bullyism, etc.

"Disagreeing with the *Richmond Whig* as to the *effect* of Sumner's thrashing, we entirely concur with it, that if thrashing is the only remedy by which the foul conduct of the abolitionists can be controlled, that it will be well to give Seward a double dose, at least, every other day, until it operates freely on his political bowels."

These passages are alike revolting to taste, decency, and morals. It is with extreme reluctance that I transcribe them on these pages. But the festering wound, periling our national life, must be probed.

The *Columbia Times*, published in the capital of South-Carolina, says: "We were not mistaken in asserting, on Saturday last, that Hon. Preston S. Brooks has not only the approval, but the hearty congratulations of the people of

South-Carolina, for his summary chastisement of Senator Sumner. Immediately upon the reception of the news, a most enthusiastic meeting was convened in the town of Newberry. The meeting voted him a handsome gold-headed cane.

"Here in Columbia a handsome sum, *headed by the Governor of the State,* has been subscribed for the purpose of presenting Mr. Brooks with a splendid silver pitcher, goblet, and stick, which will be conveyed to him in a few days by gentlemen delegated for that purpose. In Charleston, similar testimonies have been ordered by the friends of Mr. Brooks.

"We heard one of Carolina's truest and most honored matrons, from Mr. Brooks' district, say, that the ladies of the South would send him hickory sticks with which to chastise abolitionists and black-republicans, whenever he wanted them. Meetings of approval and sanction will be held, not only in Mr. Brooks' district, but throughout the State at large; and a general and a friendly response of approval will echo the words, 'Well done!' from Washington to the Rio Grande."

It is always painful to enter into the diagnosis of a malignant disease. But this is generally necessary in the attempt to effect a cure. I must therefore continue, a little further, this exhibition, revolting as it is. The *Richmond Enquirer*, Virginia, says:

"A few Southern Journals, affecting an exclusive refinement of feeling, or regard for the proprieties of official intercourse, unite with the abolition papers in condemning the chastisement inflicted upon Sumner by the Hon. P. S. Brooks. We have no patience with these mealy-mouthed Pharisees of the Press.

"In the main, the Press of the South applauds the conduct of Mr. Brooks, without condition or limitation. Our approbation, at least, is entire and unreserved. We consider the act good in conception, better in execution, and best of all in consequence. These vulgar abolitionists in the Senate, are getting above themselves. They have grown saucy, and dare to be impudent to gentlemen. Now they are a low, mean, scurvy set, with some little book-learning, but as utterly devoid of spirit and honor, as a pack of curs. Intrenched behind 'privilege,' they fancy they can slander the South and its representatives with impunity.

"The truth is, they have been suffered to run too long without collars. They must be lashed into submission. Sumner, in particular, ought to have nine and thirty every morning. He is a great strapping fellow, and could stand the cowhide beautifully. There is the blackguard Wilson*, an ignorant Natick cobbler, swaggering in excess of muscle, and absolutely dying for a beating. Will not some body take him in hand? Hale† is another huge, red-faced, sweating scoundrel, whom some gentleman should kick and cuff until he abates something of his impudent talk. Let them once understand, that for every vile word spoken against

---

* The Hon. Henry Wilson, who represents Massachusetts in the Senate of the United States.
† The Hon. John P. Hale, Senator from New-Hampshire.

the South, they will suffer so many stripes, and they will soon learn to behave themselves like *decent dogs*—they never can be gentlemen.

"Mr. Brooks has initiated this salutary discipline, and he deserves applause for the bold, judicious manner in which he chastised the scamp Sumner. It was a proper act, done at the proper time, and in the proper place. It is idle to talk of the sanctity of the Senate Chamber, since it is polluted by the presence of such fellows as Wilson and Sumner and Wade.* We trust that other gentlemen will follow the example of Mr. Brooks, that so a curb may be imposed upon the truculence and audacity of abolition speakers. If need be, let us have a caning or a cowhiding every day."

These extracts prove, beyond all controversy, that the outrage upon Senator Sumner, is not to be regarded as the act of an individual, but as the measure which Slavery, with singular unanimity, has adopted to crush free-

* The Hon. Mr. Wade, Senator from Ohio.

dom of speech in the Congress of the United States.

Slavery, vanquished in debate, makes her appeal to the bludgeon, to silence the voice of truth! And what were the particular words in Mr. Sumner's speech, which aroused such brutality? Fortunately we know exactly what they were.

The Hon. E. A. Edmundson, representative in Congress, from South-Carolina, with whom, as a friend, Mr. Brooks conferred previous to the assault, testifies on oath, before a committee appointed by Congress to investigate this matter, that the particular words to which Mr. Brooks took exception, and to avenge which he made the assault, were the following:

"Pray, sir, by what title does he indulge in this egotism? Has he read the history of the State which he represents? He can not, surely, have forgotten its shameful imbecility from Slavery, during the Revolution, followed by its more shameful assumptions for Slavery, since."

It is thus that the question has assumed an

aspect, which arouses and alarms the whole North. In order that you may compel your servants to work without wages, you must

1. Keep them in the most brutal ignorance.

2. You must enslave all the free colored people in your borders.

3. You must prevent the non-slaveholding whites in your States, from reading any books or newspapers, from hearing any lectures or sermons, which show them how Slavery dooms them to degradation.

4. You must seize our colored servants, to whom we pay wages, when we are traveling in your States, and thrust them into jail.

5. You must call upon us to help you chase your slaves when they run away.

6. You must insist that Slavery shall be established, by authority of Congress in all the free territory of the United States; and that, in defiance of our laws, you may hold your slaves in our States, bringing the code of Slavery into the States of freedom.

7. You must demand that the North shall

not, in the pulpit or the press, utter one word against Slavery, lest it should excite discontent among the "poor whites," almost equally degraded with the enslaved "blacks" of the South.

8. You must stand on the floor of the Senate Chamber, and Hall of Representatives of the United States, with bowie-knife, revolver and bludgeon, and try to overawe the advocates of freedom into silence, and into acquiescence, with all your demands.

Nay, brethren! you do even more than all this; you

9. Offer rewards for the heads of our most honored and valuable citizens, both statesmen and clergymen. Men whom all the world delight to honor, can not enter your States without exposure to the most atrocious insults and the most abusive deaths, simply because they are opposed to Slavery.

10. And, finally, you drive out of the South, by all the horrors of "lynch-law," every man who will not vote for the slaveholding candi-

date for the Presidency. You overawe the timid among you, so that they dare not open their lips; and then you, having expelled or silenced all the non-slaveholders among you, who sympathize with freedom, you, brethren of the South, numbering but six millions of citizens, all told, command us, your brethren of the North, numbering thirteen millions of citizens, to choose the President you nominate, and place the Government of the United States into your hands, or you threaten to leave the Union.

Now, gentlemen, I ask you, as candid men, can you expect us, your brethren of the North, to be very affectionate in our endearments towards you, under these circumstances! And can you deceive yourselves into the belief, that any amount of menace on your part, can now stay that flood of feeling which is rising at the North. Much as we love this Union—and we are willing to do any thing that man can honorably do for its preservation—you may depend upon it, gentlemen, that we shall not purchase its continuance, at the expense of bowing our necks beneath the yoke of Southern Slavery. You have your subject class of "poor whites" at the South. You will not create that class at the North. It is well that you should understand this. If you doubt my individual word, inquire of the Legislatures of the North, of the journalism of the North, of the Church of the North, and you will receive but one answer.

12*

CHAPTER XIII.

SLAVERY: ITS PHILOSOPHY AND ITS FRUITS.

HARDLY any thing can be imagined more dreary and depressing than a ride through the State of North-Carolina. I wonder not that Mr. Helper has raised a cry of indignation and anguish in view of the ignorance, poverty and debasement into which the State has fallen. Straggling, beggarly villages, dilapidated houses, miserable hovels, fields abandoned to weeds, degraded negroes, and ragged, pallid, half-starved-looking whites, fill up the intervals between long reaches of utter desolation. No man who has passed through the State, on the line I traveled, will say that this picture is exaggerated. I do not remember that I saw a single thrifty-looking home, a single decent school-house, or a single respectable church, from the time I entered the State until we left it. I had no time to explore the cities, where, of course, there must be indications of wealth and intelligence; and in the night we *may* have passed scenes of industry and beauty. I only describe the country as it was presented to my eye.

Here is a State containing fifty thousand square miles, being equal in area to all of New-England, with the exception of Vermont. It enjoys a warm, sunny, salubrious clime; has its mountains and its meadows; is well watered by beautiful rivers, gliding through fertile valleys. Its soil is adapted to the culture of almost every thing the inhabitants could wish to raise; it abounds in valuable forests, and in mineral ores, and ought to be the home of one of the most intelligent and prosperous people on the globe. Though thus highly favored by nature, and though one of the first settled States of the Union, Slavery has paralyzed all its energies, and it stands by the side of its dilapidated and decaying sister, South-Carolina, at the very bottom of the scale of American civilization.

The whole white population of this State, which is six times as large as the State of Massachusetts, consists of but 553,028, being more than 300,000 less than the population of the little Bay State, where the songs of freedom animate to industry. The products of the industrial arts in Massachusetts amount annually to over 288,000,000; while citizens of North-Carolina, though aided by 288,548 slaves, can produce but 9,000,000 annually. The cash value of the farms, implements, and machinery of Massachusets, in 1850, was over $112,000,000; that of North-Carolina, though six times as large, was less than $72,000,000. The value of real and personal estate in Massachusetts was over 593,000,000; that of North-Carolina, including the market price of over 288,000 slaves, was less than 227,000,000, amounting not even to one half of that of Massachusetts. In fact Massachusetts is rich enough to-day, to buy the whole of North-Carolina, lands, houses, and "niggers," and then will have enough change left in her pocket to buy the whole of South Carolina too. Indeed, according to the census of 1850, Massachusetts, after purchasing both of the States of North and South Carolina—houses, lands, "niggers," and all, will still have over $59,000,000 in her pocket, to commence paying her emancipated laborers, in advance, for their work. At least so Mr. De Bow informs us in the census, which, it is to be presumed, is correct. The tables of the census were certainly not framed with any special desire to favor the North.

In Massachusetts, there are not 2000 adults who can not read and write. In North-Carolina there are, who can neither read nor write,

1. 288,588 Slaves.
2. 27,463 Free Colored.
3. 80,163 Poor Whites.

396,114. Total who can neither read nor write.

What an appalling fact is this, that, in this one State of our Union, there are 396,114 people wallowing in this slough of ignorance. It must be with incredulity that a European receives such an account of one of the States of "free and enlightened" America. From such an appalling swamp of intellectual stagnation and pollution, the most deadly miasma must rise, and spread over the whole State. Massachusetts exported, in 1855, over $28,000,000, and imported over $45,000,000. North-Carolina, in the same year, exported less than $500,000, and imported less than $300,000. Massachusetts is braided with railroads to the amount of 1285 miles. North-Carolina, six times as large, has but 612 miles of railroad. Massachusetts has, in her public libraries, 684,015 volumes; North-Carolina, 29,592. The value of the church edifices in Massachusetts, is estimated at over $10,500,000; in North-Carolina the estimated value is less than $1,000;000.

This strange parallel might be carried still farther, but this is enough. Now, why is all this? The reply is certainly calculated to excite any one's indignation. There are, in this

SLAVERY AND ITS PHILOSOPHY. 279

State, just 28,303 individual slaveholders. They have got, in their power, 288,548 of their fellow-men, who they insist shall work for them without wages. That they may accomplish this, the whole of the rest of the State is doomed to this ignorance, beggary and shame. That 28,303 slaveholders may extort unpaid service from their fellow-men, we have the impoverishment and debasement of

1. 288,548 Slaves.
2. 27,463 Free Colored People.
3. 524,724 Non-slaveholders or Poor Whites.

840,735 Total.

Can language exaggerate the magnitude of such an outrage! You can find nothing to equal this in Austrian or Turkish despotism. A whole State is blasted; a population of over 800,000 is reduced to the condition of "niggers," and "poor whites," whom even "niggers" despise, that a little handful of slaveholders, may be exempted from paying wages to their washerwomen, their boot-blacks, and their field-laborers. And if the slaveholder persists in this determination, he *must* persist in the course he is now pursuing.

1st. He *must* keep his unpaid servants as ignorant as possible. He must close up every avenue of knowledge to their minds. If they are to be mere chattels, beasts of burden, their minds must be imbruted. Men who can read, may get hold of the Declaration of Independence — they may, perchance, understand the significance of Virginia's "fanatical and incendiary" motto, pictorial and classical, a slave rising into manhood, and exclaiming, as he crushes his oppressor beneath his heel, "Sic semper tyrannis." *This is the doom of tyrants!* It is not safe, if you would enslave your fellow-men, to instruct them. You *must* pluck out their orbs of mental vision. None but blinded men will submit to such wrongs.

2dly. The free colored people must be kept in the lowest possible debasement; and if, in defiance of all your efforts, they *will be* industrious and thrifty, and become intelligent, you *must* reënslave them, and put out their eyes also, or drive them out of your States. Men will not contentedly work in your fields without wages, live in "nigger cabins," see their sons and their daughters reduced to the level of brutes, for sale like pigs in the market, when their brethren, free men of color, are earning for themselves comfortable homes; can educate their children, and own their own wives, sons, and daughters, safe from outrage. Mississippi does wisely, Missouri does wisely, Arkansas does wisely, in voting the reënslavement of all the people of color within their borders, *if slavery is to be maintained.* Every other slave State in the Union will be compelled to follow their lead. There are two hundred and twenty-eight thousand one hundred and thirty-eight free colored people in the slave States. Their doom is inevitable if slavery's hateful voice prevails, and a deaf ear is turned to the beseechings of freedom. They can not escape. May God pity them! Many of these are industrious, Christian men; toiling meritoriously in the face of all conceivable obstacles. They are to be sold and driven by the lash to the distant plantation. Their wives, their sons, their daughters, are also to be transferred beneath the hammer of the auctioneer, to any man who has the money to buy them.

3dly. The non-slaveholders, the "poor whites," must also be guarded with equal vigilance. How long could slavery be sustained in North-Carolina, if the "poor whites" there were permitted to read Mr. Helper's book, a book which can no more be refuted than the multiplication table can be reasoned down! The poor whites must be kept in ignorance of these statistical facts. There are, already, over eighty thousand of them who *can not* read or write a word. There is another eighty thousand who *do not* read or write a word. They have, already, forgotten the spelling book through which they once toiled. But there are five hundred and twenty-four thousand seven hundred and twenty-four, in all, of these poor, half-starved whites in North-Carolina, and some of them can read, and are already looking anxiously at this subject, and inquiring if they must continue forever, to submit to this state of things. If you are determined to sustain slavery, you must bar out this light and crush this spirit. You do wisely in driving out Mr. Helper from your State! You did wisely in driving Prof. Hedrick from Chapel Hill. It is, eminently, a sagacious move, to place your own men in the post-offices, and command them not to deliver to any "poor whites" any newspaper, book, or pamphlet which can throw light upon the blessings of liberty. The danger is imminent, that these five hundred and twenty-four thousand seven hundred and twenty-four poor whites will get intelligence enough to say, We will no longer submit to this debasement and penury of our whole State, simply that twenty-eight thousand three hundred and three of our fellow-citizens, may force their servants to work without wages. You can not be too vigilant. If any man is found with the *New-York Tribune*, *New-York Post*, or a copy of Helper's book in his hands, hang him. If any one expresses the opinion that freedom is better than slavery, tar and feather him. Send your vigilance committee to the book-stores, search carefully the shelves, and if you can find that "incendiary" work there, Cowper's poems, with the "fanatical" words:

> "I would not have a slave to till my ground,
>   To carry me, to fan me while I sleep,
>   And tremble when I wake, for all the wealth
>   That sinews, bought and sold, have ever earned.
>   No! dear as freedom is, and in my heart's
>   Just estimation prized above all price,
>   I had much rather be myself the slave,
>   And wear the bonds than fasten them on him!"

If you find such "accursed abolition trash" upon his shelves, hang the bookseller at the nearest lamp-post, and burn his whole lot of "fanatical, incendiary stuff" by the hands of the common hangman. It will be a salutary caution to others. You can not sustain your institution in any other way.

The Kentucky slaveholders have just driven thirty-six industrious, worthy citizens out of the State because they disapproved of slavery. How could they do otherwise if they are determined to hold on to slavery? In Kentucky there are but 38,385 slaveholders, and there are 723,028 non-slaveholders. Now if this great mass of non-slaveholders are permitted to become enlightened, how long will they allow 38,000 men to curse the State with unpaid, compulsory toil? Gentlemen slaveholders, no one can deny your sagacity in watching over the "poor whites" more vigilantly even than you watch the slaves. Your institution has nothing to fear from the rising of the *blacks*, but you have every thing to fear from the rising of the *whites*.

The vigilance with which you exclude intelligence from the slaveholding States, proves that you are awake to the importance of this subject. The State of Massachusetts takes 8154 *New-York Tribunes*, and 1058 *New-York Heralds*. North-Carolina subscribes for 57 *Tribunes* and for 44 *Heralds*. But even this small number is deemed so dangerous, that your "vigilance committee" have ordered your post-masters not to distribute these to their subscribers. You can not allow your "poor whites" to read them.

I heard a very interesting discourse to-day, in the cars, between two gentlemen who were seated directly behind me. The one was a Southern slaveholder, who took the ground that the community should be divided into two classes, with a broad gulf between them. The one class should consist of the *laborers*, who should do the work, and be kept in ignorance; the other class should consist of the *gentlemen*, who should be highly educated and refined, and who should be supported by the toil of the laborers. "Educate the plow-boy," said he, I quote his words, "and you make him discontented with his lot." Such is the philosophy of Slavery.

On the other hand the philosophy of freedom says: "Educate the plow-boy, and you ennoble him as a man; and you ennoble his honorable calling of agriculture; you increase

SLAVERY AND ITS PHILOSOPHY. 287

his power of developing wealth from the soil;
you elevate him from a mere animal drudge to
an intellectual Cincinnatus."

Now can any man doubt which of these two
principles will most enrich and embellish a
nation, searching out its hidden resources of
wealth, rearing beautiful villages and tasteful
cottages with ornamental gardens and yards;
inciting the whole population to industry, con-
structing ships, building manufactories, invent-
ing machinery, and sprinkling the landscape
with schools and academies and colleges and
churches? Can there be any comparison insti-
tuted between enlightened Massachusetts and
the semi-barbaric Carolinas? In every conceivable thing, Massachusetts is in advance of them
both united; in painting and statuary, architecture, intellectual culture, social polish and refinement, manufactures, industrial and ornamental, agriculture, wealth, commerce, and
military power. No intelligent man can doubt,
that Massachusetts could now, in case of war,
alone, with her material and pecuniary re-
ources, overpower both of the Carolinas.

If there be any sentiment which is treason to humanity, which is suicidal to material welfare, and traitorous to the whole spirit of our institutions, it is the assertion that, by law and violence, we are to keep one portion of our countrymen debased in body and mind, that the other portion may live upon their toil. If there be any sentiment which the American should repel with infinite loathing, it is this. Shall this foul Harpy, driven from every other spot of the civilized world, which can find no resting place for its polluting foot in England, France, Prussia—not even in Austria or Russia —come and light on our flag-staff, and build its nest, and rear its young, in the folds of the stars and stripes?

We often hear it said, that gentlemen at the South can not emancipate their slaves without reducing themselves to beggary. There is some unaccountable delusion in the idea, that emancipation is the loss, the destruction, the annihilation of the laborer. Emancipation is simply an idea, a principle of political economy, which, in practice, substitutes wages for the lash. As the sun rises, on the morning of emancipation, the cotton-fields of the planter have undergone no visible change. The planters' house stands as it stood the night before. The fields are white with their beautiful, snowy garniture. The cotton-gin is there, the negro cabins are there, and even all the little ebony children, tottling about the doors. Emancipation has not broken a cart, a plow, or a hoe. It has not palsied an arm, or weakened a muscle, or impoverished a single acre of ground. The plantation is exactly as it was, not having lost one single element or particle of its wealth or productive power.

The laborers go out to work, allured by money before their eyes, instead of stripes upon their back. There is no sense, absolutely none at all, in pretending that the cultivators of cotton will be reduced to beggary, because, like honest men, they pay their laborers fair wages, as the cultivators of wheat and hay, pay their laborers, all over Europe and America. Emancipation is simply paying men wages for their work, and allowing them to work for those who will pay them best. There is nothing *destructive* in that. The slave, impelled by wages, does double work, and receives increased pay. His tact and ingenuity are cultivated; his ambition excited, and he rises from the condition of a brute, to that of a man.

A planter owns fifty negroes; and there are less than eight thousand in the United States who own more than that number. Driven to the field by compulsory labor, these negroes cost him, to feed, clothe, and house them, ten cents a day. They are lazy of course; sham sickness when they can; break every tool which can conveniently be broken, and refuse to adopt any improvements which will expedite work. The planter decides to emancipate them; that is, he introduces a new motive power to stimulate them to labor. He pays them twenty-five cents a day for their work, to be taken from the profits of his crop; allows them the rent of their cabins, and a small plot of ground for a garden, and tells them, that if they can make a better bargain with any other man, they are at liberty to do so. This is Emancipation. This is that "awful," "demoniac," "infernal," "incendiary," "fanatical" Abolition, which is assailed with such terrific epithets. One would think, from what we often hear nowadays, that the very idea of paying men fair wages, for a fair day's work, is a principle which must have come up from the bottomless pit, and could have only originated in the malignity of Satan himself.

Emancipation, instead of impoverishing the South, would instantly add almost immeasurably to its wealth. Slave labor leaves a blight on the very soil it treads upon. The average value of land in slave-cursed South-Carolina, according to the assessment of 1854, was but one dollar and thirty-two cents per acre. By a similar assessment in New-York, the land there is worth thirty-six dollars and ninety-seven cents per acre. Now, it would be far from a bad speculation for Massachusetts to buy up, as she is abundantly able to do, the whole State of South-Carolina, houses, lands, negroes and all. She could then introduce free labor, extend her free laws, and free schools, and her free Gospel, over the now benighted realm; and in the rise in the value of lands alone, she would find profit enough to pay her two or three times over for her outlay.

This is not the play of fancy; it is arithmetical deduction. The following statement by Mr. Helper, is as irrefutable as the Forty-seventh Proposition of Euclid.

"The average value of land, per acre, in New-York, is $36.97; in North-Carolina it is only $3.06. In soil, in climate, in minerals, in water power for manufacturing purposes, and in area of territory, North-Carolina has the advantage of New-York, and, with the exception of Slavery, no plausible reason can possibly be assigned, why land should not be at least as valuable in the valley of the Yadkin, as it is along the banks of the Genesee.

"The difference between $36.97 and $3.06 is $33.91, which, multiplied by the whole number of acres in North-Carolina, will show, in this one particular, the enormous loss that freedom has sustained on account of Slavery in the Old North State. Thus:

"32,450,560 acres at $33.91 = $1,100,398,499.

"A reward of eleven hundred millions of dollars, is offered for the conversion of the lands of North-Carolina into free soil. In 1850, the total value of all the slaves of the State, at the rate of $400 per head, amounted to less than one hundred and sixteen millions of dollars. Is the sum of one hundred and sixteen millions of dollars more desirable than the sum of eleven hundred millions of dollars?

"Abolish Slavery, and you will enhance the value of every league, your own and your neighbors, from three, to thirty-six dollars per acre. Your little tract, containing two hundred acres, now valued at the pitiful sum of only six hundred dollars, will then be worth seven thousand. Your children, now deprived of even the meagre advantages of common schools, will then reap the benefits of a collegiate education. Your rivers and smaller streams, now wasting their waters in idleness, will then turn the wheels of multitudinous mills. Your bays and harbors, now unknown to commerce, will then swarm with ships from every enlightened quarter of the globe. Non-slaveholding whites! Look well to your interests.

"Would the slaveholders of North-Carolina lose any thing by the abolition of Slavery? Let us see. According to their own estimate, their slaves are worth, in round numbers, say one hundred and twenty millions of dollars. There are, in the State, twenty-eight thousand slaveholders, owning, it may be safely assumed, an average of at least five hundred acres of land each—fourteen millions of acres in all. This number of acres, multiplied by thirty-three dollars and ninety one cents, the difference in value between free soil and slave soil, makes the enormous sum of four hundred and seventy-four millions of dollars—showing that by the abolition of Slavery, the slaveholders themselves would realize a net profit of not less than three hundred and fifty-four millions of dollars."

Satan is, indeed, a cruel master. He allures us to oppress our fellow-man, and then defrauds us, in this humiliating way, of the wages of our iniquity. God never deals with us so. To the above striking calculation, we must also add the perhaps still more significant fact, that the abolition of Slavery adds also to the value of the emancipated slave; for a freeman is worth, in all the calculations of national resources and power, more, surely, than two slaves. The colored people remaining on the plantation and eager to work, a docile free peasantry, are worth more to the planter, in a pecuniary point of view, the morning after emancipation, than they were the night before.

"But suppose," some one says, "a servant will not work! What shall I do then?" Do just what they do in the North, in England,

France, Germany, and all other parts of the civilized world—dismiss him, and leave him without wages. If a man will not work, neither shall he eat. "But suppose he then turns a vagrant;" the question is again asked, "What shall I do then?" Do just what they do in all other civilized lands—arrest him, place him in the house of correction, and set him to hammering stone. If he commit murder, hang him. Bring him under the power of impartial law. When all the rest of Christendom is brought under the reign of civilization and the laws, why should our Southern States remain in a state of semi-barbarism! And why should they keep our whole nation in this state of destraction, periling all our interests and happiness, simply, that they may persist in the wrong of compelling their servants to work without wages!

As we rode on, deep into the night, a gentleman entered the cars, and took the vacant seat at my side. I found him to be a very intelligent, candid man, from the State of Delaware, who deplored the evils his own State was suffering from the lingering of Slavery within its borders. In the course of conversation, I referred to the dreadful dismay and suffering which must be created by the movement now in progress throughout the slave States, to re-enslave all the free people of color, thus dooming over 228,000 of the fellow-"citizens" of Thomas Jefferson, men guilty of no crime, to eternal bondage.

"A very painful event, of this nature," he said," is now, at this hour, transpiring in my own town, in Delaware. There were two gentlemen in business in Maryland, owning, in partnership, besides other property, several slaves. After a time they dissolved partnership, and one of the firm moved from Maryland to Delaware. One of the slaves, by the name of Charles, a light mulatto, in the division, fell to the Maryland master. Charles was a very intelligent man, exceedingly efficient in the business of the firm, and by his fidelity, uprightness industry, and energy, secured to so high a degree the respect of his master, that that master, dying soon after, gave Charles his freedom.

"Charles bought him a small farm. He became a prosperous man, built him a neat house, owned a horse, a yoke of oxen, two or three cows, and fifty dollars' worth of poultry; and from the produce of this little farm carried supplies, very profitably to himself, to a neighboring market. He had a wife and four little children. Charles was a Christian. The voice of morning and evening prayer was ever heard in his dwelling; and on the Sabbath, in accordance with the usages of the Methodist persuasion, to which he belonged, he was in the habit of preaching to the colored people in the vicinity.

"Just after the Harper's Ferry alarm, a vigilance committee in Maryland, called upon Charles, and told him that ' he was too enlightened and thrifty a nigger' to be allowed to live in the State. Charles, in dismay, asked if he had committed any crime, if he had said or done any thing that was wrong, or to excite suspicion. "No," was the reply, "but it is not safe for us to have in the midst of our slaves a free nigger, as rich and intelligent as you are, and you must leave this State before such a day, or you will fare badly."

This unoffending Christian man, whose rights were thus horribly outraged, was in despair. What to do he did not know. Where to go he did not know. It was mid-winter. His crops were in his barn. How to dispose of his farm, his stock, and his crops at such short notice, he did not know. He consulted friends. They shook their heads, and said:

"Poor fellow, we are sorry for you. But we can't help you. Your presence endangers the contentment of our slaves, and you must go."

In this state of terror and perplexity Charles continued, till the day before the one on which he was warned to leave, arrived. The vigilance committee again called upon Charles, and said, in tones of menace, which almost froze the blood in the veins of the helpless man:

"Charles, if we find you here to-morrow morning, as sure as you are a living man we will hang you to the limb of that tree."

Charles, in his terror, abandoned every thing—his house, his fields, his crops, his cows, his oxen, his poultry, and, taking his wife and his four little children, fled. His alarm was so great, that he frequently looked behind him to see if his enemies were in pursuit. Not knowing where else to go, he turned his steps into Delaware, that he might seek protection of his former master, who had been in partnership with the master who had given him his freedom. It was twelve o'clock at night when the poor fugitive, with his exhausted wife and children, reached the house of the man in Delaware, from whom he hoped for protection. He rapped at the door. His former master rose, came down, opened his eyes in utter amazement, and exclaimed:

"For heaven's sake, Charles, what brought you here?"

Charles, in a few words, told his story.

"But what did you come here for?" exclaimed the man. "You can't stay here. The laws of Delaware won't allow free niggers to come into the State."

"My God! my God!" cried Charles, clasping his hands, and the tears rolling down his cheeks, "what shall I do. They threaten to hang me if I stay in Maryland. They tell me I can't stay here! Where shall I go?"

"Well," said the man, "it is a clear case that you can not stay here in Delaware. You are liable at any moment to be arrested. But there is no help for it now. You must stay here until morning."

And that was the state of the case, my informant told me, that very morning when he left his home. The gentleman who gave me this information, mentioned the names of all the parties concerned, the town in Maryland from which Charles fled, and the town in Delaware where he sought protection. I regret that I did not treasure the names in my memory.

And this is but one case out of thousands

One after another the slave States are passing laws, that if their free colored population do not leave the State, they shall be sold into Slavery; while, at the same time, they are passing laws, that if any free colored man, under any pretense, shall enter their States he shall be arrested and sold. Mississippi says to more than a thousand free men: "Leave our State before next July, or we will sell you to the highest bidder." In dismay, hoping to escape this most awful doom which can befall a man, these persecuted freemen rush, with their wives and their children, towards the frontiers of Tennessee, and Tennessee shouts out to them: "Don't you step foot on our soil. As sure as you do we will sell you into Slavery."

There are now 288,138 free colored people in peril of this doom. There are, absolutely, at this moment, while I write, over four thousand persons in terror and despair, upon whom these laws are falling like an avalanche. They look this way and that way. But escape is almost hopeless. Eternal Slavery for them and for their children, is their doom.

Poor Charles! What is to become of him? We can only breathe in anguish the prayer: "May God help him." What a story is this to be told of republican America, in England and in France! Fellow-citizens of the United States, I make my appeal to you, one and all, of all religious denominations, of all political parties, men and women—am I doing a wrong thing in presenting to you this earnest appeal, which comes from the inmost recesses of my heart, in behalf of over two hundred thousand of our fellow-countrymen, who, accused of no crime, are exposed to these woes? Are these sympathies for the oppressed, which fill my heart with anguish, and almost blister my cheek with tears, "fanatical and incendiary"? Am I the enemy of my country, because I wish to see it purified from such infinite disgrace?

The same considerations which influence one slave State to exile or reënslave the free colored people, and with many of them it must be re-enslaving, for there is no possibility of their escape, must also influence the rest. If Slavery is to be sustained, it is the general conviction that this crime must be perpetrated. Do you think it will give me pain, in a dying hour, to reflect that I have plead the cause of these my brethren? Do you think that I shall regret it, when I meet these victims of the white man's avarice at God's bar, in the day of judgment? I can not keep silence. I can afford to suffer obloquy and abuse in such a cause, yea, even martyrdom, should it be needful. What is the remedy for all these evils? It is simply for two hundred thousand slaveholders, to substitute free labor instead of slave labor. That one simple act is life and health to our whole nation. And no intelligent man can seriously reflect upon this subject and believe that there is any hope any where else.

CHAPTER XIV.

THE DISSOLUTION OF THE UNION.

As we rode through the State of Virginia, I was conversing with a Virginian, a very genial, gentlemanly, intelligent man, whose name I did not learn. The cars stopped at Petersburg, where we were to pass across the city, and take another train. A gentleman, portly in figure, well dressed, and with the air of one conscious of authority, stood upon the platform, swinging his cane. My companion immediately recognized him, and addressing him, said:

"Well! are you going to dissolve the Union here?"

"Dissolve the Union!" the Petersburg gentleman sneeringly replied. "You can not dissolve this Union any way you may attempt it. Chief-Justice Marshall said very truly, that this Union would bear a great deal before it would break."

"But I thought," my companion added, "from the noise I heard, that the Union was to be dissolved immediately."

"They are acting," the Petersburg gentleman replied, "like crazy people up at Richmond. They don't know what they are talking about. You can not find two men in the country, who can tell where to draw the dividing line. Where are we to find border States? Virginia, herself, is divided; Western Virginia for freedom, Eastern for Slavery. If neither you nor I die until this Union is dissolved, we shall live to a very old age, I assure you. The thing is impossible, utterly impossible."

So much has been recently said, and so earnestly upon the subject, that I have thought it proper to look at the question seriously. A careful general, though ever so sure of victory, will always be prepared for unexpected disasters. I have, accordingly, availed myself of every opportunity of conversing with intelligent men upon the dissolution of the Union, and of the mode, should that deplorable event occur, by which it is to be accomplished. But, I have not thus far met at the South, a single individual in favor of dissolution; neither have I met with one who could imagine any feasible plan for the rupture.

I ask, where are we to draw the dividing line? Even now, *Western* Virginia will not go with Slavery; portions of Missouri will not; and there will be nothing like unanimity in Maryland and Kentucky. And if the dissentients in these States are overpowered and dragged into a slavery confederacy, they will compose the nucleus of a freedom party, which will be continually increasing, until the Southern confederacy shall again have its free North, and its slaveholding South, as now.

And more than that, in two years after the division takes place, there will not be a slave in Maryland, Virginia, Kentucky or Missouri. Every slave will step over the border line, into the free States, unless his master sells him to the distant South. Thus it is inevitable that these border States will almost immediately become free States. Then all their interests will be with institutions of freedom. Their laws will be correspondingly framed. Emigration from the free States, will crowd over into their unoccupied lands. The determined advocates of Slavery, will follow their slaves down into the Carolinas and Florida. This effect will be accomplished by laws just as potential and infallible, as those which melt the winter's snows, and carpet the earth with summer's verdure. I have seen no man who questions this. The first tier of border States being thus emancipated, and united with the North, the same process will go on with accelerated rapidity in the second tier. It is no more in the power of man to prevent this, than he can prevent the rising of the sun.

This fact is so clear and so certain, that there

is no earthly probability, that either Maryland, Virginia, Kentucky or Missouri, would be willing to occupy the position of a border slave State. As soon as they should awake to the conviction, that the dissolution of the Union was probable, the unrelenting slaveholders would rush South with their slaves. Others would sell their slaves to get rid of them; other slaves, goaded by despair, would make the most frantic endeavors to escape to the North. The friends of freedom in these border States, would have their lips opened, and would speak loudly. They are now speaking louder and louder every hour; and their voices will not be hushed by the expulsion, in a body, of thirty-six friends of freedom from the State of Kentucky. And *then*, when the question comes to a popular vote, you will see the banner of American freedom unfurled, and these four States will wheel into line on the side of liberty. I can not think that there is an intelligent man in the United States who questions this. I certainly have not yet met with such a man.

I have inquired of several of our Senators and Representatives in Congress, if they could obtain from any of the Southern members who are there menacing disunion, any programme of their contemplated operations for a dissolution, either peaceful or revolutionary. They tell me, with one voice, that they can not draw from them the slightest exposition of any plan. When these men attempt to alarm us by the threat that they will dissolve the Union; and we reply: "The Union is bound so tightly together that you can not break the chain;" one would think that they would try to add to our terror, by showing us how they could accomplish an end, which every lover of his country must so greatly deplore. But we can not find, in newspaper paragraph, or in Congressional harangue, a word which sheds the least light upon this point. The fact is, that the moment an intelligent man begins to reflect upon this subject, he finds himself hedged about by difficulties apparently insuperable. The question was recently proposed in Congress, point-blank, to one of the Representatives from Georgia, "How will you dissolve the Union?" His reply is worthy of record:

That is a question for us to determine. We do not intend to give our enemies the benefit of the information!"

In case of Dissolution the question arises, Which party shall have the Capitol at Washington, with all its vast outlay of national buildings? Which shall have the name, "United States;" which the stars and stripes, our world-renowned flag; which the navy, the territories; and, above all, which the mouth of the Mississippi, that portal opening the commerce of the world to the most magnificent valley on the globe; a valley destined soon to surpass all other nations in population, wealth, and power?

Should the South, being in the minority, and being displeased with the action of the majority, withdraw in a body, the North certainly would not surrender to her these elements and materials of national opulence and greatness.

Should the South demand them, in whole or in part, with arms in her hands—then comes war. How are the two parties prepared to meet on the field of battle? In investigating this question we will suppose, though it is an extravagant supposition, that every slave State goes with the South. Let us look then at the resources of the

SOUTHERN CONFEDERACY.

Citizens of the South,	6,184,477
Wealth of the South,	$1,336,090,737

NORTHERN CONFEDERACY.

Citizens of the North,	13,233,670
Wealth of the North,	$4,102,172,108

In this estimate the slaves at the South are, of course, not included as property; for in the event of war they would be a fearful incumbrance. Exasperated as many of them now are, and with a terrific increase of exasperation from the movement now in progress to reënslave more than two hundred thousand free colored people, it is certain that they would avail themselves of the first hostile gun fired in the slave

States, to rise in insurrection, and that they would hasten, by hundreds of thousands, to the banners of any invading army. Would there be any hope whatever for the South in such a conflict as this? The North would exceed the South in population by 7,049,193, and in wealth by the enormous sum of $2,766,081,371. In addition to this, the North has a vast fleet, experienced sailors, and the most skillful artisans, in foundries, in ship-yards, and in all the mechanic arts. It is not speaking disrespectfully of the South to say, that, in such a conflict, her condition would be utterly hopeless.

But there is another view of this case still more instructive. Men in a passion will often do that which is exceedingly foolish, and even ruinous to themselves. We will suppose that the ultra slaveholders of the extreme South, reckless of consequences, resolve to break off from the Union, and establish a slaveholding republic. They flatter themselves that they can take Cuba and Mexico, and thus, after all, make quite a respectable appearance among the

14

family of nations. As we have shown above, the present border States can not go with them. They must immediately, or very soon, join with the North. The British provinces, which can by no consideration be induced to join the Union, now that it is contaminated with Slavery, would then find it convenient to unite with the Northern Confederacy. We are already assimilated in manners and customs, in love of liberty, in language, in religion; and our commercial and agricultural interests are identical. Montreal and Portland are friends far more affectionately united, than the capitals of Massachusetts and of South-Carolina.

What, then, would be the prospects opening before the North, should the South withdraw? The Northern Confederacy would immediately present itself before the world, in all the vigor of national power and greatness. There would be first, twenty free States, including Minnesota, Oregon, Kansas, and Nebraska, with a population of more than 16,000,000. One half of Texas, also, is certainly to be free. There would be then, in speedy union, the six British provinces, consisting of Canada East, Canada West, New-Brunswick, Nova Scotia, and Cape Breton, Newfoundland and Prince Edward's Island, including an area of 553,446 square miles, and embracing a population of 3,000,000 of freemen. We should then certainly add, within a few years at least, the five States of Delaware, Maryland, Virginia, Kentucky, and Missouri, with a population of 3,700,000 free "citizens;" for the Dred Scot decision will be dissolved in the dissolution of the Union.

Even now the slaves are being hurried out of Missouri, at the rate of one or two hundred a week. Many of the counties are already nearly drained. The *St. Louis Democrat* says, that ten years ago the slave property of the county of St. Louis, represented one twentieth of the taxable property of the county; now it is less than one ninetieth. God's providence has announced that these States must soon be free.

Thus the North would commence its career,

with a homogeneous population of more than 22,000,000 of freemen, united in every interest, and in possession of the fairest portion of the globe, for the development of mental power, and physical energy, and national wealth. Her area, sweeping across the whole continent, from the Atlantic to the Pacific, would extend North and South, from the coasts of Labrador and the frozen shores of Hudson's Bay, to the turbid Roanoke, and the mountains of Tennessee. This territory is capable of supporting hundreds of millions of inhabitants; new States would be rapidly carved out of the fertile acres of the West, and peopled by floods of emigration from the Atlantic coasts, and from the Old World.

But I hear some feeble voice say: "What will you do for shirts? You can not grow cotton in the North?" We shall do for shirts just what England does, and France and Spain, and Italy and Prussia, and Austria and Russia. We shall buy figs in Smyrna, and sugar in the West-Indies, and cotton of those who raise it.

The Canadians do not go shirtless because they are not in political union with Southern slaveholders. The South must raise cotton. It is its only possible way, while encumbered with slave labor, of getting a living. The South can not *eat* cotton, or wear the raw fabric. It must sell to those who will pay the best price. We can afford to pay as good a price as any body else.

But what can the South, as now organized, accomplish on the race-course of the nations, struggling for the supremacy in all the attainments of high civilization! The mechanic arts, now demanding the highest genius as well as artistic skill, have risen to the dignity of intellectual callings. Far higher powers of mind are now requisite in many a workshop than in the conduct of the *ordinary* labors of what are called the learned professions. It is not difficult to make out a writ, or to copy a formula. But look at the philosophical apparatus and scientific instruments of the present day; at that wondrous power of mechanism, which seems almost invested with a conscious soul; at steam-engines and locomotives; at foundries, and ship-yards, and glass factories, and potteries, and cutlery. Look at the application of chemistry and science in all the high arts. Look at architecture and civil and military engineering, in their sublime achievements; and at landscape gardening in its almost fabulous power of converting a desert into an Eden, and tell me if these works of modern civilization are to be achieved by brutalized "niggers," and almost equally brutalized "poor whites"?

Who is to perform these achievements in the benighted South, where schools are frowned down, where the plowboy and the mechanic must not be educated; where Silliman's *Journal of Science* is an incendiary sheet, which must be excluded from the State; where the postmasters are enjoined to pilfer the mails of every copy of the *Tribune*, the *Post*, and the *Times*, and to throw them into the fire? You thrust hot irons into the mental orbs of your laborers in the South, and do you think that they can compete with the clear-visioned and honored artisans of the North?

The slaveholders themselves, it is true, are to be allowed to attain to some intelligence. But will *they* build clipper ships, and construct imperial locomotives, and weave precious fabrics, and lift up domes of architecture, and span streams as with aerial arches? They are gentlemen! This is work. And, according to the slaveholding philosophy, work is degrading, fit only for "greasy mechanics." Where, then, is there any hope for the South? To sustain Slavery she must degrade labor, and shut out intellectual light. The journalism of all free lands must be excluded; no schools must be established, for it is even more perilous to educate the "poor whites," than the poor blacks. Thus, year after year, the South must be drifting rapidly towards barbarism. There is no escape.

In the mean time, our Northern ships will triumph over all seas. The neighing of our imperial locomotives, those steeds, "whose sinews are steel, and whose provender is fire,' will be heard from the Atlantic to the Pacific; our manufactories will send their products to all the nations and tribes of earth; our schoolhouses will rouse the mental energies of the whole population, and, from ten thousand farm-houses and workshops, will introduce to the homage of a grateful world new Fultons, and Newtons, and Arkwrights.

Is this fancy? Are these airy visions? Look at the South now, and see! There she is, a melancholy spectacle to the whole world, the Spain of the Western Continent; larger in area than England, France, or the North; with as salubrious a soil and as rich a clime as the sun ever shone upon. And what is she doing for the world? She is driving, with the lash, between two and three millions of lazy negroes to work, raising cotton, tobacco, and sugar. That's all! And even this, the humblest of all work, for picking cotton requires but little intellect, she does at such an enormous disadvantage, that of these crops, she does not raise one third of what ought to be raised, and would be raised, under free labor. Our shirts and our muslins cost us twice as much as they need cost us, were the fields of the sunny South tilled by the intelligence and the energies of freedom.

I do not know of a thing in which the slave-holding South is not far behind England, France, or the North. She is behind in agriculture, in commerce, in manufactures, in literature, in the fine arts. Just so fast as the South drives Slavery out of any portion of its territory, it seems to awake from its Rip Van Winkle sleep. Baltimore, Mobile, New-Orleans, are becoming free cities, and they are developing the energies of freedom. But enter any city of the South where Slavery is predominant, and free labor is not recognized, and you meet every where the genius of decay.

Brethren of the South, I do not ask these questions triumphantly or tauntingly, but sadly. Why should your beautiful fields be thus desolate? Why should you not have lovely villages and tasteful homes? Why should not

14*

commerce spread her sails in your ports, and the hum of machinery blend with the voices of your waters, and railroads embroider your fertile acres, and bridges span your streams; and your presses give to the world the literary and scientific productions of your fine minds?

Look at England. Look at France. Look at the North. How can you bear the comparison? We may indeed ask, Who reads a Southern book, or charters a Southern ship, or wears a Southern coat, or treads a Southern carpet, or visits a Southern studio for paintings and sculpture? We might continue these questions in regard to all articles of household furniture, farming utensils, carriages, harnesses and saddles, and every article of male or female dress from the hat or the comb upon the crown of the head, to the leather which protects the sole of the foot. The slaveholding States have slid away from the companionship of enlightened nations, and are still sliding down the declivity to depths whose bottom has not yet been fathomed.

It is often said, amazing as the assertion is, that the prosperity of our country depends upon the maintenance of slavery, and that the abolition of the system, and the introduction, in its stead, of the system of free labor, would impoverish our whole land, North and South alike! Such an assertion seems too absurd to be refuted. And yet let us for a moment treat it as if it were respectable, and then we will open the door and bid it begone!

Look at the assertion then. According to the last census, there were three millions two hundred thousand three hundred and sixty-four slaves in the Southern States. Mr. Dana, in his interesting work, *To Cuba and Back*, says of the slaves on a large plantation:

"Allowing for those too young or too old, for the sick, and those who must tend the young, the old, and the sick; and for those whose labor, like that of the cooks, only sustains the others, not more than one half are able-bodied, productive laborers."

Now, upon this calculation, there are one

million six hundred thousand one hundred and eighty-two able-bodied negroes at work in the kitchens, the stables, and the fields of the South. We are a nation of thirty millions of people. Is it not absurd, infinitely absurd, to affirm that the prosperity of these thirty millions, is dependent upon our compelling one million six hundred thousand one hundred and eigthy-two poor, debased, ignorant negroes to work without wages!! May we not dismiss such an impudent impostor as this assertion without any further notice? And yet this argument has been adduced in the face and eyes of that West-Indian experiment, which proves, that if you will pay these poor, defrauded men honest wages, they will do at least a third more work than they now do, impelled only by the terror of the plantation-whip. They will raise a third more of cotton, of tobacco, and of sugar. The philosophy of slavery is political economy maudlin drunk.

Bitterly as the dissolution of the Union is to be deplored, and calamitous as that event may seem to the general interests of liberty; rudely as it would shock our fraternal feelings towards thousands in the South, who are to us as brothers and sisters, still there are aspects of the question, far from unpleasant in their bearings on the North. We shall then be, slavery having been exscinded, a united and homogeneous people, with identical interests; and all our energies, state and national, will be consecrated to the diffusion of liberty and intelligence. We shall no longer feel, that we are personally degraded by a compact which renders it necessary for us to join the slave-hunters, with their dogs, in pursuit of fugitive slaves; there will no longer be any danger, that our Senators will be beaten down upon the floor of Congress, or that our nation will be disgraced by brawls in legislative halls. The dissensions which have disturbed our peace for so many years, will instantly come to an end; and the South will be no more to us then, than Cuba and Mexico are now. We shall only wish it prosperity. It can not excite an emotion of jealousy.

If any feasible plan could be devised for the dissolution of the Union, it is certain that slavery might thus be effectually abolished. It is possible that this is the plan, in the Divine Mind, for the attainment of an end so indispensable to the peace and prosperity of our land. Still there is, at the North, such a universal desire for the perpetuation of the Union, that its dissolution can only be accomplished, by the determined action of Disunionists at the South. Should they succeed, the bells which our Southern brethren will ring, proclaiming that the union between the slavery-loving South and the freedom-loving North is dissolved, will also announce, over mountain and prairie, that the doom of slavery is sealed, and that the hour of emancipation draws nigh. Those jubilations will proclaim to expectant bondmen and freemen alike, the repeal of all fugitive slave laws, and Dred-Scott decisions, those blackest blots upon the pages of the nineteenth century.

Every link in the chain of the slave, will at once be weakened. In droves they will rush across the invisible line which will then separate their Egypt from their Canaan, and they will find no weary wilderness intervening. Even now the heart of the whole North throbs sympathetically with every fellow-man, whether in Turkey, Hungary, or Georgia, who tries to shake off the shackles of bondage and rise up, a freeman. It needs but the act of Dissolution, perpetrated by the South, to rouse the whole North to enthusiasm, and to change that silent sympathy into active coöperation. Three millions of slaves on one side of an invisible line, more than a thousand miles in length, will not remain there long, when there are twenty-five millions of white men, energetic, powerful, and wealthy, whose bosoms are glowing with the love of universal liberty, on the other side, ready to receive them with open arms. We have millions of acres waiting for their hoes and spades. We shall certainly protect them; and shall honor every man, Caucasian, Mongolian, Ethiopian, Malay, or Indian, who adopts the noble principle of one of Virginia's noblest sons "Give me liberty or give me death!"

The dark border line of slavery, like an eclipse passing over the sun, will move rapidly down towards the Gulf, and the docile slaves of the South, self-emancipated, "bought without money," will spread over the limitless realms of the North, the East and the West, clasping hands with their brothers in Canada, peasant laborers, sowing our seed, reaping our harvests, aiding in all manual toil, and adding vastly to the resources, the wealth, and the luxuries of a nation of freemen, until, finally, they themselves shall be lost in that vast flood of Caucasian population, which has already either engulfed or swept before it the Indian race, and which is, doubtless, destined soon to make this whole continent ring with shouts of liberty.

It is thus certain, that the Dissolution of the Union, is the emancipation of the slave. It is possible, that this is the divine plan. Many who are called "ultra-abolitionists" of the North are so convinced of this, that they desire above all things the Dissolution of the Union, not as an end, but as the necessary and potential means for the attainment of that most glorious of all ends, Freedom in America. They rejoice in every effort which violent men make at the South in favor of Dissolution; and, with great satisfaction, repeat the ancient maxim so often illustrated in the history of this world: "Quem Deus vult perdere, priusquam dementat."*

It is very possible, that this is the Providential arrangement for the overthrow of that system of wrong and outrage, which is such a curse to our whole nation. Perhaps there is no other way in which this object can be so humanely accomplished; punishing the oppressor by leaving his fields desolate, and yet saving his family from the horrors of a servile insurrection. Much as my heart clings to this Union, if our Southern brethren will not substitute free labor for slave labor, and, if by this temporary dissolution, their families can be

---

* "Whom God would destroy, he first makes mad."

saved from the horrors of a servile insurrection, and the slave be thus led, without bloodshed, to liberty, my heart will certainly say: "Father, thy will be done."

But the appalling thought is, that, in the exasperation of the rupture, the South may provoke the North to war. The first gun would be the signal for flame and blood throughout the South. The reënslaving of the free colored population, is only furnishing the plantation negroes with intelligent leaders, men of nerve, men of Saxon blood, men goaded to desperation. May God, in mercy, avert so dreadful a doom! Fathers and mothers, the South is not a safe place in which to leave your children. There is warning in the historic words: "After us the Deluge."

And will you permit me, brethren of the South, to recall your minds to the fact, that the "irrepressible conflict" upon the subject of slavery, in which our country is now engaged, is a conflict which has originated in a change on *your* part and not on *ours?* You certainly will not deny that Washington, Jefferson, Hamilton, Madison, Franklin, all the founders of our Constitution, felt as we do now: that slavery is an evil, greatly to be deplored, entirely inconsistent with our principles, and, that its abolition at the earliest possible hour was infinitely to be desired. They merely *endured* the evil for a little time, fully expecting that it would soon come to an end. How decisive the voice of Hamilton upon this point.

"The fundamental source of all your errors, sophisms and false reasonings, is a total ignorance of the natural rights of mankind. Were you once to become acquainted with these, you could never entertain a thought, that *all men* are not, by nature, entitled to equal privileges. You would be convinced, that natural liberty is the gift of the beneficent Creator to *the whole human race;* and that civil liberty is founded on that."

Now we still entertain these same sentiments which were entertained by the founders of our republic. We have not changed our views, and are still looking for the accomplishment of that enfranchisement, which both your fathers and ours hoped and believed would have taken place long ere this. While we thus have not changed at all, the change in your principles and conduct, has been radical and awful.

You now declare that slavery is not an evil, but a blessing; that it meets with your cordial approbation; that it is divinely appointed and approved. You insist that it shall spread unobstructed through all the territories of the Union. You call in the aid of the Supreme Court to deprive colored men of their rights of citizenship, thus throwing millions of our fellow-countrymen out of the protection of the laws. You insist upon the right of spreading your slave code, so revolting to our sense of justice, over our free States, so that you may come with your slaves, at your pleasure, and sojourn among us, holding them in bondage by your slave codes, in defiance of our free Constitutions; buying and selling and flogging them in our streets, regardless of our laws. You make new laws, stringent and humiliating, compelling us to harden our hearts against our noblest instincts, and to join the oppressor against the oppressed, aiding you to catch your slaves, and rivet anew their broken chains.

These were not the views of Washington and Jefferson and their compeers. They loathed such notions, and so do we. The change is with you, and not with us. Do you think that we shall follow you into the black gulf of such principles as these? Gentlemen, we shall do no such thing. When you can raise Thomas Jefferson from the grave, and induce him to make a pro-slavery speech; or when you can call up the spirit of George Washington to declare that the desire for the abolition of slavery is "incendiary," and "fanatical," then, perhaps, may you hope for the free North to say, that ignorance is better than knowledge, that debasement is better than culture, that slavery is better than freedom.

And think for a moment, brethren, how

monstrous is your proposition, that we should allow your slave code to intrude upon our free soil, and triumph over our free institutions. If a Turk come to Portland, and, in accordance with the Turkish code, sews up his wife in a sack and tosses her into Casco Bay, he will soon find the grip of our laws upon his neck, with unmistakable evidence that he is no longer upon the shores of the Bosporus. Turkey has her local laws. We do not interfere with them. But she can not bring them to New-England. And if the Turk is dissatisfied with our laws, asserting that we are defrauding him of his "rights" by not allowing him the privilege of drowning his wives when he gets tired of them, he must stay at home. And you, gentlemen, must do the same. South-Carolina has her local laws. So has Massachusetts. South-Carolina approves of compelling men to work without wages. Massachusetts does not. South-Carolina approves of allowing a man to flog his servant when, where, and how he pleases. Massachusetts does not. South-Carolina approves of selling pretty girls at auction to the highest bidder. Massachusetts does not.

Now if a South-Carolinian wishes to do those things, he must do them at home. He can not do them in Massachusetts. If any man, with us, attempt to cowhide his coachman, or his wife's waiting-maid, we ask no questions as to where the man came from, or whether such acts be lawful in his own country, be it Turkey, Madagascar, or South-Carolina. He has violated *our laws*, and must go to the house of correction. South-Carolina is at perfect liberty to establish such laws as she pleases, *at home*. But, like the Turk, she must leave them at home. She can not bring her local laws to Massachusetts, and with them override ours.

Will you deny the correctness of this principle? You do deny it with audacity which is marvelous You claim the right of bringing Slavery into lands of freedom, of blasting the green sward of Bunker's Hill with the blight of Carolinian bondage; of annulling, on our own soil, our own laws, and substituting yours in their stead. Should we yield to such a claim we should deserve to have the collar placed upon our necks, and to be driven to the cotton-fields beneath the cracking of the plantation whip.

And what will be the condition of the South? It will consist of eleven States, with but 3,347,-148 free white inabitants. A large portion of these are "poor whites," degraded by Slavery to a position almost below that of the slaves. There will also be within her borders, a dark and frowning band of over three millions of slaves, ever menacing insurrection, and ever eager to grasp the bludgeon and the knife, to avenge the yet unavenged wrongs of ages. Now what can the South do under these circumstances? Compared with the North she is but a child in a giant's hands. Can she take Cuba? Even Spain would laugh the fillibustering expeditions of such a nation to scorn. Could she annex Mexico? England has but to say, "I prefer that you should not," and the South will not dare to raise a finger. Think of the desolation in the South, should England land a regiment of blacks, supported by a few thousand white troops, and proclaim liberty to the slaves. And even could the South annex Mexico, what is it but an annexation of ignorance, confusion, and semi-barbarism, which would drag the South even lower into the gulf of national impoverishment than she now lies.

Gentlemen of the South, matters have gone so far that it is time that we should look at this question seriously. I have earnestly tried to get some idea of the plan of Disunion, contemplated by those Southern gentlemen, who profess themselves to be so eager for the rupture. I have inquired in Washington, I have asked my friends to inquire. I have scrutinized speeches in Congress, and in Southern conventions, and have read Southern journals, but all in vain. I can get no reply whatever.

Now I have presented to you the picture of the Dissolution of the Union as, after many inquiries and long and careful reflection, it presents itself to my mind. Should this expose induce you to present your plans, it would gratify a wide-spread curiosity. But the elements to be combined, in the two confederacies then to be organized, are so distinctly defined, that, though you may modify some of the minor details, it is not possible that results should ensue essentially different.

Truly I can not see, much as I should deplore disunion, that it would be any serious calamity to the *material welfare* of the North. On the contrary, there are obviously some advantages, which the North would reap from such a measure, compensating, in no small degree, for the disappointment we should feel in the severance of so many at the South, whom we love as friends. Among these advantages are:

1. The Slavery question would with us be settled at once and forever. All the slaves would be immediately withdrawn two or three hundred miles farther South, and that question would be at rest. We should then have no more to do with Southern Slavery than we

now have to do with Cuban Slavery. Our friends at the South can hardly conceive what a relief this would be to our minds.

2. We should then be a homogeneous, united, affectionate people ; united as Massachusetts and New-York are, as New-York and Ohio. We could travel any where over our whole country, without being exposed to the danger of "Lynch Law." We could express our opinions freely in the cars, and read what books we pleased. And should any citizen of the United States be insulted in Cuba, in Mexico, or in the Slaveholding Confederacy, we could preserve our self-respect by sending an army to avenge the insult, and to prevent its repetition.

3. We should no longer be in political alliance with a large class of men at the South, whom we abhor. There are many at the South whom we love, but many whom we detest. There are those at the South, who attempt to intimidate our Senators and Representatives, by the bludgeon of the assassin ; there are those

who shout hosanna to the wretches who perpetrate such crimes; there are those who offer rewards for the heads of our most respected statesmen and revered divines; there are those who are continually insulting us with threats that they will "Dissolve the Union," unless we obey their commands, bowing our necks, with the negroes, beneath the plantation-whip. We endure fellowship with such men, only from our attachment to those residing among them, who are different. It would grieve us to be separated from our friends; but there would be great comfort in being able to say to those who are not our friends: "We withdraw from you our national fellowship. Henceforth you shall be to us but as Cuban men, and as Mexicans."

4. We should escape that infinite mortification which we now encounter when traveling in foreign lands. Throughout Christendom, Slavery is the great disgrace of the United States. I was once traveling on the Rhine. An Austrian gentleman, seated by my side, learning that I was from America, inquired:

"Is it really true, my dear sir, that in America they sell men, women, and children, in the markets, as we do pigs? And is it true, that bloated debauchees can buy pretty, Christian girls at auction—for—for—for what they call *fancy girls?*"

"Yes, sir," I replied, "it is!"

And I added not a word, about "The queen of the world, and the child of the skies," or about "The land of the free, and the home of the brave."

Should this Union be dissolved, I shall wish to go to Germany immediately, and hunt up that Austrian officer, and entice him to ask that question again. How would my heart exult in saying:

"No, sir; thank Heaven, no, sir! My country is the land of liberty, not of Slavery. The stars and stripes float over a nation of freemen. Slaves can not breathe in America.

'If their lungs
Receive our air, that moment they are free;
They touch our country, and their shackles fall.'"

5. We should have no more disgraceful squabbles in Congress, expending millions of money in quarreling over the Slavery question; our mails would no longer be pilfered in searching for papers, or pamphlets, or letters, advocating freedom. Our political journals could circulate as free as the winds which sweep our hills and prairies. The only element of national discord would be removed, and having once doubled the stormy cape of Disunion, our national ship, with all her canvas spread, would bound over the billows of Pacific seas.

Such are the advantages the North would find in Disunion. "Why then," some one inquires, "is it not best to adopt this measure? We are so strong at the North, we can cut off the South, if we please. If the limb be so diseased that it can not be cured, amputation had better be performed."

It certainly would be much better to adopt this measure, than to live in such a state of warfare as now exists. But when we remember, that there are only two hundred thousand men who make all the trouble; and, that if any power of "moral suasion" can be brought to bear upon them, so that they can be induced to pay their laborers honest wages, all our discord is at an end, it does seem absurd that this Union, formed with so much care, and promising such blessings to the world, should be dismembered through the avarice and the folly of such a trivial band of mischief-makers. We cling tenaciously to the Union, ever hoping that this obstacle to our progress, so contemptible in its character, may soon be removed.

I once heard of a train of cars being stopped by grasshoppers. They lit in such numbers upon the rails, that, crushed by the locomotive, they so greased the track, that the ponderous engine could not move. The obstruction, real as it was, struck every one as supremely ridiculous. Shall the United States of America be arrested in their glorious career, by two hundred thousand slaveholders who insist upon flogging instead of paying their servants? It is ridiculous.

There is no foundation, whatever, for the notion, that the millions of intelligent, energetic, enterprising freemen, the hum of whose industry rises like an anthem from all the States of the North and the West, are dependent for their prosperity upon political union with a few thousand slaveholders, who drive some million and a half of negroes to unpaid toil. England is in prosperity, France is in prosperity, Canada is prosperous, though not politically connected with the slaveholding States of the South. And so might the free North be in a state of prosperity such as she has never known before.

Indeed, in case of dissolution, I can hardly conceive it possible that war should arise. The North never threatens disunion; never thinks of withdrawing. It is the South alone which deafens the ear with these menaces. They threaten to withdraw from the United States. Surely they do not expect to drive the North out of the United States. If the South, a feeble and impoverished band, in the extreme minority, abandon us, they can not, Samson-like, drag the Capitol and the territories, and the Navy, with them. The material wealth of the United States remains where it was, subject to its executive authority. Will those in revolt demand a share of this wealth? We shall say: "It belongs to the United States, and we have neither the right nor the inclination to surrender it to any body." Will they endeavor to wrest it from us by force? It would, indeed, be "Quixotic Chivalry," even for six millions of people, to provoke the ire of thirteen millions; particularly when these six millions are encumbered by three millions of slaves, watching for an opportunity to rise, and march to freedom through a *Red Sea*. You would not attack us, brethren of the South. And we should not attack you. You would have nothing which we should want.

You sometimes speak of the attachment of your slaves for their owners, and intimate that, in case of war, you could arm them to fight your battles. Surely, you will not expect intelligent men to accept this statement. There are, of course, cases in which waiting-maids are attached to kind mistresses, and in which colored nurses love the white children they tend, as well, perhaps even better, than their own; and in which body-servants are attached to indulgent masters. But, from these individuals, turn to the million toiling upon the plantation, who seldom see their owners, and who are smarting beneath the lash of the overseer. Do they love their masters? Will they fight to rivet their chains, and to drive off those who would lead them to freedom?

These are the real slaves of the South. They are becoming more exasperated every day. The movement now in progress to reënslave two hundred thousand American freemen, is accumulating in this outraged band, energies of exasperation which are appalling. Many a freeman, whose little home has been broken up; whose wife and children have been torn from him, and who has been driven back upon the plantation, there to toil in life-long

Slavery, is goaded to madness. His hour of vengeance will come! And terrible will it be. Who can blame him?

No! the South has nothing to hope for, from the slave, in the event of war; nothing to expect but desolation, flames and blood. The South would be even more helpless in the hands of the North, than Mexico would be now struggling against the whole power of the United States. How suggestive upon this point, are the following observations made by Mr. Helper:

"Look, now, to the statement of a momentous fact. The value of all the property, real and personal, *including slaves*, in seven slave States, Virginia, North-Carolina, Tennessee, Missouri, Arkansas, Florida, and Texas, is less than the real and personal estate, which is unquestionable property in the single State of New-York. Nay, worse; if eight entire slave States, Arkansas, Delaware, Florida, Maryland, Missouri, Mississippi, Tennessee, Texas, and the District of Columbia, with all their hordes of human merchandise, were put up at auction, New-York could buy them all, and then have one hundred and thirty-three millions of dollars in her pocket. Such is the amazing contrast between freedom and Slavery in a pecuniary point of view. When we come to compare the North with the South, in regard to literature, general intelligence, inventive genius, moral and religious enterprises, the discoveries in medicine, and the progress in the arts and sciences, we shall, in every instance, find the contrast equally great on the side of Liberty."

A separation from associates who do not love us, who disapprove of our religious and political principles, who are continually calling upon us to do that which we can not do without shocking our sense of right—such a separation would, undeniably, relieve us from many embarrassments, and would remove an incalculable amount of friction from the machinery of our government. And yet I have no personal acquaintance with a single man in all the North, who would not deplore the event of a dissolution of the Union as a great grief. We have very dear friends at the South. We are allied to the South by many ties, having stood shoulder to shoulder on the field of battle to win our independence. We want to cling together in fraternal and righteous union. We feel that the difficulty which now alienates us, formidable as it is, is not an insuperable difficulty, and that upon the removal of that obstacle, we can come together with one heart again, the most free, the most prosperous, and the most happy people upon the globe.

I had just completed the last paragraph, when I chanced to open the *New-York Times*, and read the following item of intelligence:

"Forty-three negroes, who have been expelled from Arkansas, under the terms of the recent Legislative enactment, which prescribed that, in the event of their non-departure, they should be sold into slavery, arrived in Cincinnati, January 2, in a destitute condition. They were met by a committee appointed for the purpose, by the colored population of Cincinnati. It is reported that the upward-bound boats upon the Mississippi are crowded with these fugitives flying from their homes."

Is not this infernal? Can such scenes occur in Christian America, in the nineteenth century, and not rouse the indignation of God? Slave State after slave State, is passing these atrocious laws, dooming their whole free colored population to exile or slavery. More than two hundred thousand of our fellow-countrymen, guilty of no crime, and accused of no crime, are menaced with these woes. Already many thousands are breasting the storms of winter, and are attempting to escape to the North. Mothers are flying in terror, leading by the hand, or carrying upon their backs, their infant children. In unutterable dismay these poor fugitives have abandoned their homes, and, shivering with cold, and starving with hunger, and fainting from exhaustion, are striving to escape the most dreadful doom which can befall a mortal—endless slavery. But few can escape. The journey is long. The winter is cold. They have no money. Infants, the sick and the feeble must perish by the way. Many confined by the sick or the dying can not even attempt to escape. In despair they must remain and bide their doom. O God! O God! where shall these outraged children of thine look for help!

Are we, fellow-countrymen, "Fanatics," "Incendiaries," and "Enemies of the South" because our souls bleed in every fiber through sympathy for these sufferers? There are millions in our land who will continue to feel for them, and pray for them, and plead their cause. Menaces can neither turn their hearts into stone, nor silence their lips. They will not be intimidated by threats of dissolving the Union, or by any display of bludgeons, stakes or gibbets. Christianity, at the North, is aroused and will never again be silenced. The heart of philanthropy is throbbing, with pulsations beating heavier and heavier. Literature has lifted up her warning voice, and political economy has uttered her indignant cry. The doom of slavery is sealed. May God grant that the execrable institution, the last relic of barbaric ages which still lingers among us, may speedily go down; but not in a sea of flame and blood.

www.ingramcontent.com/pod-product-compliance
Lightning Source LLC
Chambersburg PA
CBHW030304240426
43673CB00040B/1060